Living
and INSIDE OUT
UPSIDE DOWN

We thank God
for you and your
being used of the
Lord to bless us.
May He reward
you as you
live for Him

Rich & Carolyn
too

Mary Jean

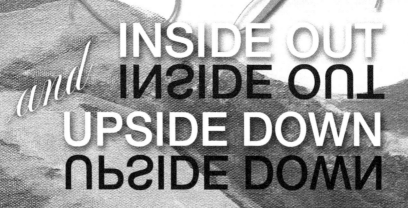

Living

and INSIDE OUT
UPSIDE DOWN

A JOURNEY THROUGH
THE SERMON ON THE MOUNT

Richard L. Hagenbaugh

XULON PRESS

Xulon Press
2301 Lucien Way #415
Maitland, FL 32751
407.339.4217
www.xulonpress.com

Paperback ISBN-13: 978-1-66288-198-5
Ebook ISBN-13: 978-1-66288-199-2

Dedication

This study is dedicated to
Carolyn Rae Peters Hagenbaugh

She believed in me and encouraged me
when I needed it the most, and many times since.

and
to my children, the love of my life,

RaeLynn Hagenbaugh Stenchever
and
Richard Darryl Hagenbaugh

Who became the training ground
that grew me in so many of these truths.

Acknowledgment

My thanks to
MarJean Peters
generous with her time
and gracious in spirit
Cover Design
By
MarJean Peters

Purpose

The German theologian, Dietrich Bonhoeffer, once said the following about the Sermon on the Mount (Matthew 5-7): *Humanly speaking, it is possible to understand the Sermon on the Mount in a thousand different ways. But Jesus knows only one possibility: simple surrender and obedience, not interpreting or applying it, but doing and obeying it. That is the only way to hear His words. He does not mean for us to discuss it as an ideal. He really means for us to get on with it.*

You have to love the quaint way Bonhoeffer says, *Get on with it.* That becomes the challenge for every 21st century Christian. When Jesus gave us the Sermon on the Mount, He intended a new code for life, a new method for living, and a new ethic from what the world had ever known. That brings me to the purpose of all this gathered material. It is possible to read a book, and when finished, you put it down and think no more about it or its content. However, from the beginning, it has been my purpose for people to return to this material repeatedly.

It is a little like maintaining a heart condition. You think about it every day and take the medication daily to stay well. Furthermore, you act differently. You do nothing that might aggravate your condition. This dominating issue determines all you do and wherever you go. That is how the Sermon on the Mount should look for the Christian. Experience has taught me that the only way to live out the principles of the Sermon on the Mount is to know it so well that it becomes second nature.

One book in my library I read once a year, whether I need it or not is <u>*The Knowledge of the Holy*</u> by A.W Tozer. It is marked and worn. Furthermore, I have given away dozens of these books. That should be our relationship with the Sermon on the Mount. Please read it and interact with the principles often. Then, make resolutions to do certain things that will align you with the will of the Lord Jesus as contained in His most powerful, meaningful, and, I might add, current sermon.

In this sermon, He tells them something incredible. They must live their lives from the *Inside Out*. He takes the laws of the Pharisees and says something must take place on the inside first before anyone can keep those laws. To live out the reality of this sermon, we must live our lives, *Inside Out and Upside Down*. Everything starts in the heart, the attitude, and the mind. That may feel strange because it goes against our nature. On the one hand, we might feel like we are Inside Out or Upside Down. But on the other hand, we will look just the way God wants to see us live.

This project has been a work in progress for many years. I am thankful for all the available resources quoted in the material. I pray it will help strengthen the Christian community, especially those who are new to the faith and those struggling to live out their faith wherever it is seen or studied. I firmly believe the 21st-century church must become effective in evangelism and conversion growth. The only way for that to happen is for something dynamic to occur in the hearts of those already saved. The implementation of and obedience to the Sermon on the Mount will do just that. May God bless and grow you as you study and interact with this material.

*D*R. Hagenbaugh takes us on a journey through the packed, crucial teaching of the Sermon on the Mount. In easy-flowing prose, he helps the reader understand and personally apply Jesus' teaching on living righteously before a loving and holy God. We desperately need the teaching of the Sermon on the Mount to stand for the Lord Jesus in an age carefree about what is right and true. This book gives much-needed help.

–– Terri Williams, ThM,
Wheaton College, Retired Missionary, WorldVenture, Professor,
Church History.

IN His Sermon on the Mount discourse, Jesus sets the attitudinal and behavioral bar high for those who follow Him. Pastor Rich, a master word crafter, and storyteller, boldly exposes the notion of "easy believism," and brings this challenge to Christians–– *to take our Master seriously by endeavoring to live a righteous life in the power of the Spirit.* Jesus the Messiah is neither militant nor monastic but rather a gentle shepherd of souls. Rich does not hint of legalistic pressure but calls us to a grace-enabled path of discipleship, where Cross-empowered righteousness in the inner man results in righteous actions of the outer man. Hagenbaugh's work is theologically rock solid. As a veteran pastor well-experienced with the fallenness and flaws of real people, Rich "brings it" with a comprehensive understanding of who Jesus calls us to *be.* Commenting on the «narrow gate,» he calls the question more relevant today than ever: *will we cave into the pressure of current worldly culture or choose to walk the path of the kingdom counter-culture Jesus invites us into?*

–– Tom White
President, City Advance; Founding member of Global
Cities Alliance;
Author, *The Believer's Guide to Spiritual Warfare*

FILLED with practical wisdom, Dr. Richard Hagenbaugh presents insightful commentary on the Sermon on the Mount. He provides a readable and informed guide to help Christians grasp important theological and practical matters. Read to benefit from Hagenbaugh's years of pastoral experience.

–– Neal F. McBride
Retired Professor of Psychology and Chaplain, Colonel, USAFR.

WHAT could be more useful today than a work that grounds us in the rules and guidelines for life that lead to unrelenting fullness and deep satisfaction? In a time when many struggle to understand the basics of living well in the Kingdom of God, Hagenbaugh's deep exploration of the Sermon on the Mount brings to light, timeless truths that change everything. Both a scholar and practitioner; Hagenbaugh's words compel us to follow the way of Jesus, and the invitation is just as strong through his life,

–– Josh Carstensen
Senior Pastor, Northwest Hills Community Church,
Corvallis, Oregon

FROM serving in the local church alongside Richard Hagenbaugh for three decades, I can say this book is "vintage Rich." Without compromise, it seeks to reveal the truth in Christ's sermon, not glossing over the difficult sayings or lowering the bar regarding a kingdom citizen's walk of obedience. Devoted attention to Old Testament background, helpful explanation of key Greek words, and consistent application to everyday living characterize this book. I especially appreciated his careful exposition of the passages on divorce and remarriage, which is worth the book's price. This book will work well as a discipling tool and greatly aid personal growth.

—Brian Newcombe
ThM, Western Seminary, Retired Pastor

I'VE known and respected Pastor Rich for years and appreciate his wisdom and teachings consistently based on the Word. His insights bring a fresh perspective and depth. They are seasoned, wise, grounded in the Word, and deserve our time, attention, and application. His decades of research, teaching, and familiarity with Greek and Hebrew are condensed and crystalized for us to absorb. For those with too much to do and too little time to do it, this book is an excellent distilled source of wisdom worth every minute spent.

— J.J. Haberman, M.D.

AS a man of God's Word, Pastor Rich wisely communicates and applies the gospel and openly shares how he receives its correction. He often guides us to the original Hebrew, Greek, or Aramaic words and translations with practical applications. Despite a tough childhood, Pastor Rich chose to forgive, overcome, and seek identity in God! He freely shares his story and inspires listeners to overcome lies, take them to God and follow Him. One Sunday, Pastor Rich shared about stopping his message to first apologize to his son for losing his temper the day before. That is a man of God!! Pastor Rich humbly showed how God's Word directs us to work in a community context. We fell into a comfortable habit of isolating ourselves from the church and needed someone to challenge us to lay our self-sufficiency at the cross. Richard and Carolyn openly, honestly, and intentionally involve themselves in the church community. We deeply love, appreciate, and pray for them daily. We call them for wise counsel and guidance in our marriage and family. Pastor Rich continues drawing us to relevant Scriptures that lay the path forward. The genuinely mature man of God is wise, humble, and happy to come alongside others in their time of need. Our whole family treasures our times with Pastor Rich and Carolyn.

–– Higgins Family

Table of Contents

Chapter 1

The Value of the Sermon on the Mount:

At one time, I was a fire department member in Sandy, Oregon, District 72. I enjoyed my relationship and opportunities for ministry with the men in the department. One of the first things they gave me was a large book entitled *Firemen's Basic Training Course.* I took the book home and never opened it thinking I might learn all I needed from the other men and the experience. After all, on-the-job training is the best.

Pages 28-30 of this manual explain what to do when a fire truck rolls up at a fire. There are always two men on the back of the truck, and one jumps off at the hydrant pulling the hose off the truck and wrapping it around the hydrant. Then the truck goes on to the fire while the man at the hydrant fits the hose to the hydrant for the main water supply.

One day I was at the fire station when the alarm went off and we all jumped into our gear and headed to the fire. I ended up in the back of the truck. When the truck stopped at the hydrant, I jumped off just like I was supposed to. However, no one ever told me I was to take the hose, wrap it around the hydrant, and then hook it up. So, I jumped off and shouted to the driver. He proceeded to the fire and all the hose went with him and the rest of the crew. You should have seen us scrambling to get water to that pumper.

I did not read the manual, and the result could have been tragic. The Sermon on the Mount is the manual for Christian living during the kingdom and the ordination sermon for the twelve disciples. Beyond that, it describes the commission for every Christian who goes out to fulfill Christ's life and work. In this sermon, Jesus gave the blueprint for living in the kingdom of God. Even though this sermon was probably given shortly after the choosing of the twelve, it involves the official summation of the teachings of our Lord.

It is a wonderful thing that God has given us so much of His word. We have the Prophets, Poetry, History, Epistles, and much information about future things. However, if we had nothing else besides the Sermon on the Mount, we would have enough information to live the kind of life on earth which God wants us to live during the kingdom. Therefore, this sermon does not repeal the Mosaic law but states the principles behind it. It is not a series of rules to protect society but to develop the individual himself to fit into the kingdom's society. Naturally, therefore, it does not contain truth on the substitutionary death of Christ, His resurrection, the doctrine of justification, or the plan of salvation.

Dr. James T. Fisher, a veteran psychiatrist, made the following statement: *If you were to take the sum total of all the authoritative articles ever written by the most qualified of psychologists and psychiatrists on the subject of mental hygiene, if you were to combine them and define them and cleave out the excess verbiage, if you were to take the whole of the meat and none of the parsley, and if you were to have these unadulterated bits of pure scientific knowledge concisely expressed by the most capable of living poets, you would have an awkward and incomplete summation of the Sermon on the Mount.*

Jesus gave us the Sermon on the Mount so that we would know how to live our lives in a way that pleases God. He would not be with us for our whole time on earth, and He needed to give significant instruction so we might properly live for Him. Christian teaching is always far more than merely giving information about a way of life. A deep concern for the person who hears it dominates it.

There is a story that Leonardo da Vinci's career began when his sick teacher asked him to finish a painting that the teacher had begun. Da Vinci protested that he could not do it. The teacher said, "Do your best." Da Vinci did his best, and when he finished, the teacher saw it and exclaimed, "My son, I paint no more." Our Lord wanted to inspire His earthly disciples so that it would not be necessary for Him to be on earth in the flesh anymore.

The Kingdom:

The kingdom embraces all created intelligence in heaven and on earth who willingly subject themselves to God, and thus, remain in fellowship with Him. The "Kingdom of Heaven" describes any rulership God may assert on the earth at a given period. The Kingdom of Heaven is the time in which we live right now. The Sermon on the Mount teaches us how to live in that kingdom and just how to please God in the process.

The "Kingdom of God" and the "Kingdom of the Heavens" are linguistic variations of the same idea. The Kingdom of Heaven is a term used by Matthew because he did not wish to offend the Jews to whom he wanted to communicate the Gospel. The term is used 33 times in Matthew.

We have said the kingdom is any time God rules. Therefore, God rules in people's lives right now, making us part of the kingdom. The final fulfillment of the kingdom will come when the Lord Jesus Christ reigns on earth for 1,000 years.

The Sermon on the Mount may well be called the Millennial Kingdom's constitution. Israel rejected this sermon and the miracles of Jesus from chapters 8 and 9. This rejection led to the discourse in chapter 13 about the mysteries of the kingdom. This discourse refers to the intervening time between His rejection and the second coming. This further shows that the Sermon on the Mount is for today's Christians.

Some History:

People have recognized the Sermon on the Mount as one of the most remarkable and significant statements of moral and spiritual truth. However, at the same time, it has been history's most debated sermon. Some have contended that it is too unrealistic, while others contended it is legalistic, belonging to the tribulation period or kingdom age. Count Tolstoy approached it with a wooden literalism applicable to society and consequently advocated the abolition of all police establishments and armies. On the other hand, Thomas Aquinas believed only the religious orders in the monastery and convent should fully comply with this sermon. Both were wrong.

Who are the Addressees?

In the main, our Lord addressed His disciples (5:1-2). This included the twelve, but undoubtedly includes a larger group (4:23-25).

The present tense indicates that Jesus intended the sermon for the present. No statement occurs which puts the application into the future. The Beatitudes ("Blessed *are* you"), the descriptions of influence ("You *are* salt"), the commands ("take heed that you *do*"), and the instructions to ("pray") are all in the present tense, which refers to the present, and to us as Christians in any day. The mention of a kingdom keeps entirely with the present-day, spiritual kingdom.

Though not every statement in the Sermon on the Mount is in the Epistles, no requirement in the sermon is in disharmony with church truth. We can find everything in the sermon in another form in the Epistles; very little indeed that is not found implicit and explicit in those written by Paul while he was a prisoner in Rome.

Why Study the Sermon on the Mount?

The Lord Jesus died to enable us to live the Sermon on the Mount. We should study it because nothing shows us any more vividly the absolute need for the new birth and the indwelling Holy Spirit's work. This sermon crushes me. It showed me my utter helplessness and undoing were it not for the new birth in my life.

We must study it, and as we do, we must face ourselves in the light of it. Facing ourselves will drive us to see our ultimate need of the rebirth and the gracious operation of the Holy Spirit in our lives.

Easy Believism:

The truth of the Sermon on the Mount exploded in the minds of those who heard it because of their reluctance for Jesus to evaluate their standing before God by His strict standards. Unfortunately, such reluctance is also present today. Now an atmosphere of "easy believism," allows people to experience initial happiness with the Gospel, but not a deep, long-term joy derived from serious obedience to Christ's commands. Jesus knew about easy believism; we did not invent it. He spoke to the issue in John 8:30-31.

You might be saying, "Well, I am a Christian. I believe. I made a decision for Christ." Many people point to the past to verify their salvation, but did you know the Bible never does that? It never points to the past but always bases proof of real salvation on your life in the here and now. "Examine" in I Corinthians 11:28, for instance, is in the present tense imperative, "Be constantly examining yourself."

How do you examine yourself? Look at Matthew 5. When Jesus arrived, the Jews had already decided what right living was about. They had developed their own code and system of holiness. It was all external, self-righteous, and based on works. Jesus shattered that when He said, "I want to give you a new standard of living, a new criterion by which to evaluate whether or not you are redeemed." He told them how a true citizen of the kingdom lives.

The Need for Righteousness:

Do you want to prove yourself? Then let the Spirit of God compare your salvation to facts in the Sermon on the Mount. Here is the standard: the key is one word, "righteousness." Jesus says, "If you are a child of the King, your life will characterize righteousness."

Recently, a friend told me a man in his church had been living with a woman who was not his wife. Is he a Christian? That is certainly a fair question. I Corinthians 6 says fornicators do not inherit the kingdom of heaven. Why? Because fornication is unrighteousness, and true conversion characterizes righteousness. Christians can commit fornication, but when they do, we cannot distinguish them from non-Christians. Therefore, it is fair to question their salvation.

This sermon's key verse is in Matthew 5:20. *For I say to you, that unless your righteousness surpasses that of the Scribes and Pharisees, you shall not enter the kingdom of heaven.* They went to the temple daily, paid tithes, fasted, and prayed. They were religious freaks!

However, Jesus says our righteousness must surpass theirs. Therefore, righteousness is the issue. It is the one thing that sets us apart as converted people. Righteousness means living right and under God's standards, by His definition. If we do not live this way, the genuineness of our salvation is open to suspicion by others and to ourselves (usually in the form of insecurity).

Hebrews 12:14 should haunt anyone claiming to be a Christian and whose life does not match that claim. *Sanctification without which no one will see the Lord.* II Timothy 2:19 says, "The Lord knows those who are His." Who are they? Those who name the name of Christ and depart from iniquity.

Titus 1:16 says, *they profess to know God, but by their deeds they deny Him, being detestable and disobedient, and worthless for any good deeds.* Therefore, profession means nothing without obedience, righteousness, holiness, and departing from iniquity.

John MacArthur once heard a pastor say, "Isn't it wonderful you can come to Jesus Christ and don't have to change anything on the inside or outside?" Can that be true? Never! There had better be transformation. Of course, we come to Jesus just as we are, but if we come away from conversion just as we were, how can we call it conversion? II Corinthians 5:17 sums it up nicely: *Therefore, if any man is in Christ, he is a new creature; the old things passed away; behold new things have come.*

The Sermon on the Mount tells us how to live right and be righteous in a world where people will not see righteousness otherwise:

> Right Attitudes (5:1-12)
> Right Words (5:33)
> Right Worship (6:1-18)
> Right Relationships to material things (6:19-34)
> Right Relationships to People (chapter 7)

The world can see that you are distinct, characterized by a hunger for righteousness, resulting in right thinking, talking, acting, worship, and relationships to money, the things of this world, and people.

You say, "Who could ever live like that?" The question is good, and I am glad you are asking it. The fact is no one can live like that. Only the one born again and filled with the power of the Holy Spirit can live like that. When we place our faith and trust in Jesus Christ, He saves and converts us into a new creation.

God is patient. God is kind. God is good. God is gracious. God is merciful. God is longsuffering. God is not willing that any should perish. Nevertheless, God's mercy has its limits. Therefore, if you have not committed your life to Christ and come into the kingdom on His terms, you had better do it while you can. Come to the light while the light is available. Come to the Son while He shines.

Review and Resolve:

1. What is the primary purpose of the Sermon on the Mount?
2. Why does Matthew use the term "Kingdom of Heaven" and what is the definition of the term kingdom?
3. Why do we believe that this sermon is meant for modern day Christians?
4. How does this sermon combat the "Easy Believism" of today?
5. Write, in your own words, the key verse of the Sermon on the Mount?

Chapter 2

The Reward of a Nobody

And when He saw the multitudes, He went up on the mountain; and after He sat down, His disciples came to Him. And opening His mouth He began to teach them, saying, 'Blessed are the poor in spirit, for theirs is the kingdom of heaven.' (Matthew 5:1-3)

General William Booth, the founder of the Salvation Army, defined the problem in today's Christianity well when he said: *I consider that the chief dangers which will confront the twentieth century will be:*

Religion without the Holy Spirit
Christianity without Christ
Forgiveness without regeneration
Morality without God, and
Heaven without hell.

To many, Christianity is like a Christmas tree. They go out and cut or purchase a beautiful little tree and take it into their home, where they decorate it with lights, tinsels, and many other things. But all the beauty comes from what they tack onto the tree. On the other hand, consider the apple tree. It is rooted in the soil; it breathes the air; it is warmed by the sunshine and watered by the rain. Life nurtures the inside of the tree, and, in due season, blossoms cover the branches, and eventually, the fruit comes. As we study the words of Christ in The Sermon on the Mount, we realize that life begins inside the person and overflows into his attitudes and actions in life.

Five Good Reasons for Studying the Sermon on the Mount:

1. Because it shows the necessity of the new birth. We can never please God by ourselves or by using the flesh. The only people who will know blessedness are partakers of the divine nature. The Sermon on the Mount strengthens the Law of Moses by showing us the need for salvation. It gets right to our attitudes and says we cannot live even one day of blessedness without Jesus Christ and the new birth.

2. It clearly points to Jesus Christ and perhaps is the single most significant insight into His mind. It teaches us how our Savior thinks.

3. It is the only way to happiness for Christians. If you want to be happy and filled with the Spirit of God, don't seek some mystical experience or an elusive dream. Master The Sermon on the Mount.

4. It is the best means of evangelism I know. If we ever really live out the Sermon on the Mount, we will blow the world away for Christ.

5. It pleases God. That is a high privilege. It is a beautiful thought that sinful people like you and me could please God.

Six Discourses (Sermons given by Jesus):

There are six long discourses which Jesus spoke, of which the Sermon on the Mount is one:

The Sermon on the Mount (Matthew 5-7). This deals with the moral and ethical principles of the Kingdom. This is a detailed revelation of the righteousness of God and its principles.

1. Sermon Commissioning the Twelve (Matthew 10:5-42).
2. The Discourse on the Present age (Matthew 13) talks about the mysteries of the Kingdom while the King is absent.
3. The Upper Room Discourse (John 13-17). Here Jesus discusses the church as the body of Christ in the present age.
4. This involves the concerns of the Kingdom (Matthew 9:35-10:42).
5. The Olivet Discourse (Matthew 24-25). This is Christ's teaching on the end of the age.

Jesus and the Multitudes:

Verse 1 of Matthew's introduction says, *And when He (Jesus) saw the multitude.* The multitude always moved the Lord Jesus, and He was concerned for them. (Matthew 9:36, 14:14, and 15:32), explain that Jesus saw the multitudes and had compassion on them.

Verses 23-25 in Matthew's fourth chapter describe this multitude. Jesus was going about Galilee teaching in the synagogues, preaching the gospel of His Kingdom, and healing the sick. His fame had spread everywhere, and *great multitudes followed Him from Galilee, Decapolis, Jerusalem, Judea and beyond the Jordan.* They came from the north, south, east, and west, and when Jesus saw them, as always, it broke His heart. When He saw them hungry, He gave them food. When He saw them sick, He healed them. When He saw their spiritual hunger, He reached out to them and met their spirit's needs.

Crowds came after Christ: sick, demon-possessed, Pharisees, Sadducees, Essenes, Zealots, ritualists, harlots, publicans, scholars, illiterates, refined, degraded, rich men, and beggars. There was no class or rank when it came to following Jesus.

Jesus had great compassion for all these people. Perhaps we learn a lesson from Him here. Jesus directed His compassion to the unlovely and often unwanted people! The church today must learn this lesson. Far too often, we direct our compassion toward ourselves, our nice clothes, and modern-day worship. Christ's ministry was to the undesirables so should ours be.

Jesus Sat Down:

It is essential to notice that Jesus was seated when He spoke to the people because that was the traditional way for a rabbi to teach. When He sat and talked, the whole speech was official from a rabbinic point of view. That's true even today. When a professor is given an assignment at a university, we give him "the chair." The Roman Catholic Church tells us that the Pope speaks "ex-cathedra," ("from his chair").

What Jesus was saying was not some random thought; it was the official manifesto of the King. *And opening His mouth"* is a colloquialism in Greek, used to describe solemn, grave, dignified, serious, and weighty statements. This phrase is also used in some extra-biblical references to speak of someone sharing intimately from his heart.

Progression in the Beatitudes

It is easy to observe a sequence or progression in these Beatitudes. We see first the poor in spirit, which is the right attitude toward sin and leads to mourning in verse 4. After you have seen your sinfulness and mourned over it, you are met with a sense of humility. Then you seek and hunger and thirst for righteousness. That is then manifested in mercy (v. 7), in the purity of heart (v. 8), and in peacemaking (v. 9). The natural result is that people revile, persecute, and falsely accuse you. By the time you have lived out the Beatitudes, you have become sufficiently irritating to the world, and they will persecute you.

It is essential to note the division in these verses. Matthew 5:3-6 are the "be attitudes." Matthew 7:1-12 represent the "do attitudes."

Blessed:

The word we begin with is "blessed." Scholars also translate this word as "happy." Translators used this word to describe the gods. The term "blessed" literally means an inner joy that is untouchable by the world. When the Christian has God within his soul, nothing on earth can touch him. It is not the same as human happiness. "Happy" is built on the word "hap," which literally means: "chance." Human happiness often depends on the chances of life, over which a man usually has no control. A sudden illness, a deep disappointment, or the loss of some material blessing are a few things that can change happiness into sorrow. "Blessed" describes that joy which has its secret within itself, that joy which is serene, untouchable, and self-contained, that joy which is entirely independent of all the chances and the changes of life. Jesus later refers to this as blessedness when He says, *Peace I leave with you, my peace I give unto you: not as the world gives, give I unto you. Let not your heart be troubled, neither let it be afraid"* (John 14:27).

This next "blessed" is very clear. Blessed are those whose spirit is destitute. Blessed are the spiritual paupers, the spiritually empty, the spiritually bankrupt who cringe in a corner and cry out to God for mercy. They are the happy ones.

This truth is not just in The Sermon on the Mount. We find it in other places in the Bible:

James 4:10, *Humble yourselves in the presence of the Lord, and He will exalt you.*

Moses describes Jacob's night fight in Genesis 32.

Isaiah, Isaiah 6:5, *Woe is me, for I am ruined! Because I am a man of unclean lips... for my eyes have seen the King.* At that point, God blessed him.

Gideon, Judges 6:15

David, II Samuel 7:18

Peter, Luke 5:8

The world says, "Assert yourself, be proud of yourself, and get all you can." But God says when you admit your weakness, your nothingness, that is not the end but the beginning of real blessing. However, it is the hardest thing you will ever do.

The Kingdom of Heaven

Theirs is the kingdom of heaven. This is a grand pronouncement of something already theirs. The pronoun is emphatic, "Theirs alone." The kingdom "IS" theirs. The verb is in the present tense. It is not just something for the Millennium, but for right now. The reign of Christ is now. Happiness is now.

The Kingdom is a society where we do God's will as perfectly on earth as in heaven. That means only he who does God's will is a citizen of the Kingdom. We can only do God's will when we realize our utter helplessness, ignorance, and inability to cope with life and put our whole trust in God. The Kingdom of Heaven is the possession of the poor in spirit because they realize their helplessness without God and learn to trust and obey.

Becoming Poor in Spirit

We must become "poor in spirit" to see the Kingdom of Heaven. So, the application of the message is that we are "poor in spirit." But how does that happen?

First, do not try to do it yourself. That was the folly of monasticism. These people thought they could be poor in spirit by going somewhere, selling all their possessions, putting on a crummy old robe, and sitting in a monastery. It doesn't work that way. Looking at yourself or even at others will not do it. The place to look is to God.

In his book *The Sermon on the Mount*, Arthur Pink says to starve the flesh. By this, he means to starve the carnal nature. Even some Christian ministries and ministers in this generation seem to feed on pride. We must seek things that strip the flesh naked.

Finally, we receive poverty of spirit in a very simple way. ASK! Do you want it? Ask God for it as the Publican did, "Be merciful to me." Jesus said that man went home justified. Happy is the man who is a beggar in his spirit. He is the one who possesses the Kingdom.

Review and Resolve:

1. Give two favorite reasons for studying the Sermon on the Mount.
2. What was Jesus' attitude toward the multitudes?
3. What lesson is there for us in His attitude toward the multitudes?
4. What is significant in that Jesus sat down to teach the people?
5. Define "Poor in Spirit."
6. Resolve to do one thing this week in order to become "Poor in Spirit?"

Chapter 3

Comfort for Those Who Mourn

"Blessed are those who mourn, for they shall be comforted."
(Matthew 5:4)

All around us, many refuse to come before God and grieve over their sin. Aaron Burr was one of those people. Remember that Burr was vice-president of the U.S. from 1801-1805 and he had actually conspired with Timothy Pickering to pull New York out of the Union and create a new union with New England. Burr's differences with Alexander Hamilton came to a head in 1804 and he challenged Hamilton to a duel. The two men appeared early on the morning of July 11, 1804, under Weehawken Heights on the New Jersey shore of the Hudson River, where three years later, Hamilton's son Philip would be killed in a duel arising out of politics. Hamilton shot in the air; Burr shot his opponent through the body. Hamilton died two days later, and the Vice-president fled New York from an indictment for murder and the storm of anger his act raised.

The granddaughter of Aaron Burr gave her heart to Christ in an evangelistic meeting. That evening she said to her grandfather, "I wish you were a Christian, too."

He replied, "When I was a young man, I went to an evangelistic meeting. I felt my need of God's mercy and forgiveness and knew I should give my heart to Christ, but I walked out without doing it. I stood under the stars and looked up toward heaven and said, 'God, if you don't bother me anymore, I'll never bother you.'" Then he told his granddaughter, "Honey, God has kept His part of that bargain. He has never bothered me. Now it is too late for me to bother Him."

A misspent life, filled with deception and treason against the United States, followed Aaron Burr's fateful decision.

The Paradox:

Something is fascinating about this Beatitude since it also translates as *Happy are the unhappy.* This translation seems contrary to everything we know in life. Jesus did that frequently. He gave us something that goes against our knowledge and expectations. The whole structure of our life, the pleasure madness, thrill seeking, money, energy, time, enthusiasm expended in seeking amusement and entertainment are expressions of the world's desire to avoid mourning, sorrow, and pain. And yet, Jesus said, *Happy are the unhappy!* Therefore, in His offer of a new approach to life, Jesus condemns the laughter and happiness of the world. He pronounces blessing, happiness, joy, peace, and comfort on those who mourn.

There are nine words in Greek alone (all used in the N.T.) to describe the concept of grief indicating it is part and parcel of living. The whole of human history overflows with tears and sorrow, but we haven't seen anything yet, according to Matthew 24. There is an Arab proverb which says, "All sunshine makes a desert!" Someone else has said, "The triumph song of life would lose its melody without its minor keys."

The ancients used an interesting little instrument called the "Tribulum" to beat grain to divide the chaff from the wheat. The word "tribulation" comes from this word. Tribulations truly separate the chaff from the wheat in human character.

Different Kinds of Sorrow:

The First, is General Sorrow, the sorrow of life, a proper type of sorrow acceptable as usual weeping, mourning, and part of life. Did you know the ability to cry is a gift of God? Our pain and anxiety can poison our entire emotional system if we do not release it in tears. We see this kind of sorrow in the following illustrations:

- Abraham wept when his wife died. They were tears of separation or death.

- In Psalm 42:2-3 the psalmist mourns as his soul pants after God with tears of loneliness.

- In II Timothy 1:3-4 Paul says Timothy wept tears of discouragement and defeat.

- Jeremiah 9:1 says that the prophet came to Israel and preached with tears of disappointment.

- Acts 20:31 is where Paul admonished people with tears of concern.

- In Mark 9:24, a father's tears of compassion ran for his demon-possessed son.

- In Luke 7, a woman washed Jesus' feet with her tears and dried them with her hair. They were tears of devotion, worship, and heartfelt gratitude. Love can make people cry. Jesus wept at the grave of Lazarus because he loved him and over Jerusalem because He loved its people.

The Second Kind of Sorrow or mourning is improper and illicit. We see this in the following:

- When a man mourns because he cannot satisfy his lusts, as in II Samuel 13, Amnon wept until he was sick because he wanted to defile his sister, Tamar.

- Ahab mourned because he wanted Naboth's vineyard, and we are told in I Kings 21:4 that he mourned so much that he would not and could not eat.

- There is foolish, extended mourning when people cannot let somebody go. When a person dies, a loved one becomes an emotional basket case.

- There is illicit sorrow because of overdone guilt. II Samuel 15-20 records Absalom's attempt to dethrone his father, David. When Absalom dies, his father grieved so much that his soldiers were ashamed they had won the battle (II Samuel 19:6). David's love is admirable, but his idea, stupid. Who wants proud, egotistical Absalom to run Israel? So why was David sorrowing like that? Perhaps because of guilt over having been such a terrible father and hoping his sorrow would wash his soul from his failures.

The Third Sorrow:

None of that, however, is what Jesus means here. He is talking about godly sorrow that differs significantly from healthy or unhealthy mourning. Paul helps us to understand what Jesus means in II Corinthians 7:10: *For the sorrow that is according to the will of God produces a repentance without regret, leading to salvation; but the sorrow of the world produces death.* You can cry your eyes out about your problems, weep all you want about loneliness, discouragement, disappointment, and out of sincere love, and you can cry your head off about your unfulfilled lusts. None of that worldly sorrow will bring life when it is all done.

Only one kind of sorrow brings life: godly sorrow that leads you to repentance. Therefore, Jesus is referring in this Beatitude to sorrow over sin. That is the issue, and it directly relates to the Beatitude which precedes it. So, first, there is spiritual bankruptcy and knowing it. That is the intellectual part. Then, there is weeping or mourning over that spiritual condition. That is the emotional part.

After David's terrible sin with Bathsheba, and making sure Uriah, her husband, was murdered, he said it was only in sin his mother conceived him. He was hopeless and poverty-stricken (Psalm 51). He mourned so profoundly that it wrenched his soul to its very depths.

What Jesus Means by "Mourning:"

The word "mourning" *(pentheo)* which Jesus used in this Beatitude, is the strongest, most severe of all nine Greek words used for grief in the entire New Testament. It is reserved for mourning the dead and was used of Jacob's grief when he believed Joseph, his son, was dead (Genesis 37:34). It is used in the gospels, in Mark 16:10, for example, after the death of Christ when ... *those who had been with him... were mourning and weeping.* The word conveys the idea of a deep inner agony, not just an external wailing. Scripture well illustrates this concept:

- David, Psalm 32:3-5: *When I kept silent about my sin, my body wasted away through my groaning all day long. For day and night Your hand was heavy upon me; my vitality was drained away as with the fever-heat of summer. I acknowledge my sin to You, and my iniquity I did not hide; I said, 'I will confess my transgressions to the Lord'; and You did forgive the guilt of my sin.*

- Psalm 51:1-3, David reflected on the same sin with Bathsheba and said: *Be gracious to me, O God, according to Thy lovingkindness; according to the greatness of Thy compassion, blot out my transgressions. Wash me thoroughly from my iniquity and cleanse me from my sin. For I know my transgressions, and my sin is ever before me.*

- Psalm 32:1-2: *How blessed is he whose transgression is forgiven (the man who has mourned) whose sin is covered! How blessed is the man to whom the LORD does not impute iniquity.*

The Result for the Mourner:

Mourners are happy because they are the only ones God forgives. The rest of the world was to live with endless guilt. But get it straight now––happiness does not come from mourning; it comes from God's response to it.

They shall be comforted. Who shall comfort them? *Paraclatos* is the Greek word from which we get our English "Paraclete." It refers to one who is called alongside or a comforter. References to God as a comforter fill the Bible (Psalm 30:5 50:15; Isaiah 55:6-7; Micah 7:18-20). Jesus was a comforter in John 14:16. God is said to be *The God of all comfort* (II Corinthians 1). And the Word of God is also a comforter in Romans 15:4. When comforted, we are truly happy. Happiness comes to sad people, not because they are sad, but because their sadness leads to comfort. I love what Jesus said in Matthew 11:28: *Come to Me, all who are weary and heavy-laden, and I will give you rest.*

It comes down to this: We have comfort for as long as we mourn and confess our sins. Then we can genuinely rejoice because Jesus lifts the burden of our sin.

Mourning and Repentance:

No man can repent unless he is sorry for his sins What really changes men is when they suddenly come up against something which opens their eyes to what sin is and what sin does. A boy or a girl may go his or her way and may never think of the effects and consequences of their choices; and then one day, something happens, and that boy or girl sees the stricken look in their father's or a mother's eyes; and suddenly they see sin for what it is. That is what the cross does for us. As we look at the cross, we will say, "That is what sin can do. Sin can take the loveliest life in the world, make an absolute mess out of it, and smash it on a cross." One of the great functions of the cross is to open the eyes of men and women to the reality and horror of sin. And when a man sees sin in all its horror, he cannot do anything but experience this intense sorrow for his sin.

Mourning and the World:

You know what the world says about all this! "Pack up your troubles in your old kit bag and smile, smile, smile!" However, the Bible says, "mourn, mourn, mourn!" There is not enough mourning over sin in our world. Notice James 4:8-10: *Draw near to God and He will draw near to you. Cleanse your hands, you sinners; and purify your hearts your doubleminded. Be miserable and mourn and weep; let your laughter be turned into mourning, and your joy to gloom. Humble yourselves in the presence of the Lord, and He will exalt you.*

There is no greater message for the world, or for that matter, for the church. We must be people who mourn over our sins. It must grieve the heart of God to see the frivolity and the foolishness that goes on in the name of Christianity. Nobody ever entered the Kingdom of God without mourning over his sinfulness. But unfortunately, we are grieving over less important things. We lament about starving people or those taken hostage, earthquakes, and the cost of fuel. But do we mourn over sin in our society?

I fear the church today has a defective sense of sin. So many people think the Christian life is a joke, that the church is something to laugh at and make fun of. As a result, we in the church believe we may continue in the most immoral sin and remain right with God and the church. And then, there are the people who have set themselves up as satiric critics of the church and spend their time thinking of funny ways to comment on Christianity.

Television often portrays evil, and Christians laugh. Sometimes we laugh when someone acts in unethical ways and at ungodly jokes. We must ask ourselves, "are those things laughable? Proverbs 2:14 says that some delight in the perverseness of evil. II Thessalonians 2:12 warns against rejoicing in iniquity. Do we do that? We must not!

These principles are not saying we should not have fun. On the contrary, the Old Testament is clear when it says a merry heart does good, like medicine. But we are so out of balance. We take that medicine all the time! It is a far cry from mourning over our sins and the sin of our society and culture.

The New Testament never tells us Jesus laughed. I am sure He did, but the Scriptures do not tell us He laughed. They tell us He experienced hunger, thirst, and anger, and He wept, but it never says He laughed. Somehow, we have lost sobriety. When you think about it, Jesus did not have much to laugh about. He came to die for our sins. Yet, an entertaining, thrill-seeking, pleasure-mad, silly world of fools, jesters, and comedians suck us into their vortex. But Jesus was a man of sorrows and acquainted with grief. That is what it means to mourn over sin. Even Jesus mourned over sin (other's sin).

The Scars Remain:

Can you understand we must mourn over and deal with sin? If we do not, comfort and happiness will escape us. Furthermore, the consequences will never go away. There was a woman, who in her childhood, had a fiery temper. Often, she said unkind things to the people around her. One day, after an argument sent one of her playmates home in tears, her father told her he would drive a nail into their gatepost for each thoughtless, mean thing she did. Whenever she did a kindness or a good deed, he would withdraw one nail.

Months passed, and each time she entered their gate, those ever-increasing nails reminded her of the reasons for those ever-increasing nails until finally, getting them out became her greatest challenge.

At last, the wished-for day arrived with only one more remaining nail! As her father withdrew it she danced around proudly, exclaiming, "See, Daddy, the nails are all gone." Her father gazed intently at the post as he thoughtfully replied, "Yes, the nails are gone, but the scars remain."

Sin is very much the same. The scars of sin remain with us for a lifetime and will continue to affect our lives. The effectiveness of our ministries for Christ may even be less as a result.

What about you? Will you mourn your sin today? Even we Christians must mourn over our sins!

Review and Resolve:

1. Can you give an example of a general sorrow?
2. Can you give an example of an improper and illicit sorrow?
3. What is the result of Godly Sorrow?
4. What is the significance of the word Jesus uses here for "mourn?"
5. What is one of the significant purposes of the cross as stated in this lesson?
6. Write down one of the scars that remains in you as a result of sin.
7. Resolve to do one thing this week that will help you mourn over sin.

Chapter 4

The Claim of the Gentle

Blessed are the gentle for they shall inherit the earth
(Matthew 5:5)

I once heard a new believer say he needed an "easy religion." The incongruity of his statement amused me. An easy religion! He should not have become a Christian if he wanted an easy religion. That is a little like being a bartender at a Baptist Sunday School picnic or a comedian at a funeral. He came to the wrong place.

Our prior studies on the Sermon on the Mount should have clarified this. Christ intended his statements to teach, among other things, that the kind of life He requires is impossible for men to live. And it remains impossible until men first come to Christ, acknowledging they cannot live it and asking Him to live it in them. The poor in spirit are blessed, not the proud. And the comfort Christ promises is for those who first mourn for their sin and the sin of others.

At this point, Jesus makes His description of the happy life even more difficult. He shows the way of blessing is also through gentleness. *Blessed are the gentle; for they shall inherit the earth.* According to Jesus, it is the gentle, not the haughty, forward, arrogant, or aggressive, whom God blesses. This statement must have shocked those who listened as utterly foreign to their way of thinking.

> They knew how to be spiritually proud.
> They knew how to be self-sufficient.
> They knew how to play the pious role.
> They knew religion.
> They were excellent with form.
> They thought they were the "in" group.
> They thought they could survive on their strength, wisdom,
>   might, and resources.

When the Messiah came, they expected Him to usher them into His kingdom, commend them on their religiosity and spirituality, and say God was well-pleased with them.

They did not understand the revolutionary approach which Jesus was preaching. He undermined all their spirituality with the first words which came out of His mouth. First, He called for a broken spirit, a mourning heart, and now added gentleness. No self-righteousness or spiritual pride would do here.

Our society is like theirs. We think the victory of the spoils belongs to the strong. Go get it! Gusto! Macho! Get all you can while you can! Perhaps we are as shocked by Jesus' new approach as were the Jews.

So, God's plan was not what the Jews thought it would be, and when Jesus started talking the way He did in the Sermon on the Mount, you can imagine their rejection. "What kind of messiah is this? What kind of a crowd is He going to collect? Who wants a bunch of sob sisters, a bunch of gentle people? They will never handle Rome!" As a result, they hated Him because He disappointed them and did not fulfill their expectations. They missed the whole point. They didn't know for what purpose He came. Humility and self-denial characterized Him and needed to distinguish all those included in His Kingdom.

They couldn't believe it then, and sometimes neither can we. We think God needs superstars––high, mighty, rich, and famous. It has never been that way. Our Lord came and hit them right where they were. He said, "Look, do you want to be in My Kingdom? The ones in My Kingdom are spiritually bankrupt, mournful, and gentle."

Poor in Spirit and Gentle:

Please note these are different, although the root word is the same. Some places in the Bible use these words interchangeably, but there is a beautiful distinction. Broken in spirit focuses on my sinfulness, and gentleness focuses on God's holiness. In other words, I am poor in spirit because I am a sinner, and I am gentle because God is so holy in comparison. Broken in spirit is negative and results in mourning, and gentleness is positive and results in seeking righteousness. That is the beauty of the sequence of the progression in the Sermon on the Mount. First, comes brokenness, the tremendous sense of sinfulness. But without despair because you begin to see the other side of it. You see a holy God and begin to hunger after His holiness.

The Zealots were saying, "We want a military messiah." The Pharisees were saying, "We want a miraculous messiah." The Sadducees were saying, "We want a materialistic messiah." And the Essenians were in the corner saying, "We want a monastic messiah." But Jesus said, "I'll give you a gentle messiah."

Gentleness in the Scriptures:

Many of Paul's New Testament letters parallel this teaching:

> Ephesians 4:1-2 – *I therefore, the prisoner of the Lord, beseech you that you walk worthy of the vocation wherewith you are called, with all lowliness and gentleness.*

> Titus 3:2 – *Speak evil of no man, to be not brawlers, but gentle, showing every consideration for all men.*

> Colossians 3:12 – *Put on a heart of compassion, kindness, humility, gentleness and patience.*

God's standard has always been the same. Gentleness is seen in the Old Testament as well:

> Psalm 22:26 – *The poor will eat and be satisfied; Those who seek Him will praise the LORD. Let your heart live forever!*

> Psalm 25:9 – *He leads the humble in justice, And He teaches the humble His way.*

> Psalm 147:6 – *The LORD lifts up the afflicted.*

God has always identified with the gentle, who are His priority. They are His kind of people:

> Isaiah 29:19 – *The afflicted also shall increase their joy in the LORD.*

What does it really mean to be Gentle?

It is essential to know gentleness comes from hearts that are poor in spirit and mourning over their sin. If you have difficulty being gentle, ask yourself if you have the other two qualities. The dictionary defines gentleness as "deficient in courage." However, that is *not* the Biblical definition. Scriptural gentleness comes from the meaning of the Greek word for "mild, gentle, and soft." The King James Version translated this word, "Meek" as a gentle person who is mild, tenderhearted, patient, and submissive. Gentle is often used to describe a soothing medicine, a gentle breeze, or a broken and domesticated colt. It is also a characteristic of Jesus. II Corinthians 10:1 and Matthew 21:5 talk about the gentleness of Christ.

Gentleness is not weakness. Instead, it is power under control. We must understand that definition – Power under control! One primary use is for a domesticated animal trained to obey commands and respond to the reins. It is the word for an animal that has learned to accept control. It is a by-product of self-emptying, self-humiliation, and brokenness before God. It is the taming of the lion. It does not mean the strength is gone from the gentle. It only means the strength is under control.

John Bunyan said, "He who is already down cannot fall." There is nothing to lose. A gentle person never defends himself because he knows he doesn't deserve anything. He never gets angry about what others do to him. He is already broken in spirit over his sin, and he is already mourning and weeping over the consequences of it. So, he humbly stands before a holy God, and has nothing to commend himself.

We see gentleness in the following men and passages:

- Genesis 12. **Abraham**: Abraham said to Lot, *You take whatever portion you want, and I'll take what is left,* even though God gave the covenant to Abraham.

- **Joseph**: He showed gentleness when his brothers came to Egypt and appeared before him, asking for food.

- I Samuel 26, **David**: He did not kill Saul when he could, although Saul deserved killing.

- II Samuel 16, **David**: Would not act in his own defense.

- Numbers 12:3, **Moses**: He was gentle above all the men on the face of the earth. Even when God wanted to make a new nation out of him, he would only pray for the people.

- Philippians 3:3, **Paul**: He could put no confidence in the flesh.

- Philippians 4:13, **Paul**: *I can do all things through Christ who strengthens me.*

The Result of Gentleness:

- **The gentle are blessed.** Do you want to be happy? That is what you will be if you are gentle. Not happiness in the world's flippant, circumstantial kind of happiness, but happiness in God's terminology, an abiding, true joy, based on an eternal relationship with the living God.

- **The gentle shall inherit the earth.** Christ means that when you enter the kingdom, you come into the original inheritance of domination over the earth that God gave to Adam. It is paradise regained. Notice the pronoun is emphatic, as in the other Beatitudes. *Blessed are the gentle, for they* only *shall inherit the earth. Inherit* means "to receive an allotted portion." It is in the future tense, meaning we will be there as part of the kingdom. We are going to reign with Jesus Christ in the Millennial Kingdom.

Gentleness is Necessary Because:

- **It indicates our salvation.** Psalm 149:4 says, *He will beautify the afflicted ones with salvation.* God will not save you if you do not come to Him with a broken spirit, mourning over your sin in humility before His holiness.

- **God commands us to be gentle.** Zephaniah 2:3 commands that we *Seek humbleness.* If we are not humble/gentle, we disobey God.

- **We cannot receive God's word without it.** James 1:21 says, *In humility receive the word.*

- **It is a witness for Christ.** 1 Peter 3:15 says, *Give an answer to every man that asks you a reason for the hope that is in you with gentleness and reverence.*

- **It brings glory to God.** 1 Peter 3:4 says if you want to glorify God, don't take care of your outside, but adorn your inside with gentleness.

How to Know if You are Gentle:

- Examine your heart. Do you exhibit self-control? Do you get angry, react, or retaliate only when God is dishonored?

- Do you always respond humbly and obediently to the Word of God? If you are gentle, you will.

- Do you always make peace? Gentleness forgives and restores. That is why Ephesians 4:2-3 says we are to be characterized with all lowliness and gentleness, endeavoring to keep the unity of the Spirit in the bond of peace.

- Do you receive criticism well and love the people who give it? Gentleness does. Do you instruct with gentleness?

Review and Resolve:

1. How did Jesus' coming and teaching conflict with the Jewish ideas of a Messiah?
2. What interested you the most about the sketch of Jewish history given in this lesson?
3. Name the four different factions or parties that were on the scene when Jesus came.
4. How does "Poor in Spirit" relate to being "Gentle?"
5. Define Gentle from a Biblical point of view.
6. Give three reasons why gentleness is necessary.
7. Give three ways to know you are gentle.
8. Resolve to do one thing this week that will help you become gentle.

Chapter 5

Blessed is the Starving Spirit

Blessed are those who hunger and thirst for righteousness, for they shall be satisfied (Matthew 5:6).

I must make a necessary clarification here. People ask, "Are the truths in the Beatitudes the rules on how you get into the kingdom, or are they rules on how you live once you are in the kingdom?" The answer is "YES." Both. To enter the kingdom, one must be poor in spirit, mourn over sin, come in meekness, and hunger and thirst after righteousness. Then, once you are in the kingdom, you continue doing the same. There will be times when we are less faithful and sometimes downright disobedient to these elements of kingdom life. But they are still a part of our lives.

Jesus says happiness is brokenness, happiness is mourning, happiness is gentleness, and happiness is hungering and thirsting after righteousness. Notice how the result of each of those fit together. "Theirs is the kingdom of heaven; they shall be comforted, inherit the earth, and shall be satisfied." Isn't that wonderful? If we sum that all up, we receive everything there is!

Hunger and Thirst:

When Jesus speaks of hunger and thirst, He talks about a great and intense desire. The force of His words is powerful, particularly in that culture. A working man in Palestine ate meat only once a week, and in Palestine, the working man and day laborer was never far from the borderline of real hunger and actual starvation. Few of us in modern life conditions know what it is to hunger or thirst. When we think of thirst, we think of simply going to the available source when we want something to drink. When we say we are hungry, we mean it is 1:00 p.m. and we are used to eating at 12:15.

The Greek verbs Jesus uses are compelling and refer to being needy and suffering from deep hunger and genuine and desperate thirst. Remember, this is not the requirement only of the one coming into the kingdom but also the pattern of the one already in it. Lenski says: "This hungering and this thirsting continues and, in fact, increases in the very act of being satisfied." It is a moment-by-moment way of life."

Illustrations from Scripture:

Let me use Moses as an illustration. God called him when he had been living in the land of Midian and saw God in the burning bush. When he went back to lead the people out of Egypt, he saw God's hand in the plagues and the parting of the Red Sea. Moses saw God as they moved, guided by the great Shekinah glory of God in the heavens. He saw God providing water to drink and manna to eat. After he built the tabernacle in obedience to God, he said, *God, I want to see your glory.* Moses had a genuine hunger and thirst for his God.

The word Jesus uses for righteousness literally means *to be right with God.* It is very akin to the word translated *to justify.* Real happiness comes from being right or in the right relationship with God.

This righteousness points to two things:

- First, it talks about **SALVATION.** Someone who hungers and thirsts after righteousness seeks salvation. He sees his sin, rebellion, and separation from a holy God. He is broken, mournful, and meek and wants

God to restore him. He wants forgiveness, and senses hunger and thirst after the righteousness of being saved. It is a desire for freedom from self and sin, its power, its presence, and its penalty. Therefore, there is a hunger to be cleansed from sin by the blood of Christ. We might read, *Blessed are those who hunger and thirst for salvation.* Interestingly, Isaiah repeatedly equates righteousness with salvation (Isaiah 45:8; 46:12-13; 51:5; 56:1; 61:10).

This issue is where the Jews of Jesus' day got hung up. They were trying to gain salvation through their works and many today try the same thing. They believed they had already attained righteousness. However, Jesus says, "Until you are flat on your back, hungering and thirsting for the true righteousness that you can't earn, you will never know what it is to be happy."

- The second element is **SANCTIFICATION.** When we hunger and thirst for righteousness as Christians, we want the sanctification of increased holiness. I do not know how to express this as strongly as I feel it, but I hope there is in my life this hunger that never stops, the desire to be more and more like Christ. This hunger is the mark of a genuine Christian. We keep hungering and thirsting to desire more virtue, a greater purity. We never get to the place where we think we have arrived, which is a tragic attitude for any Christian. Notice what Paul says in Philippians 3:13-14, *Sons of the kingdom never stop hungering.*

God does not finish His work in us until we leave earth. Therefore, no matter how much we love, we should love more. No matter how much we pray, we ought to pray more. No matter how much we obey, we ought to obey more. No matter how much we think like Christ, we should think like Christ more. Blessed are those who continually hunger and thirst for righteousness.

Righteousness in Bits and Pieces

There is a further consideration here that comes from Greek construction. The text tells us that we do not seek parts of righteousness but all righteousness. It does not say, "I hunger for a piece of bread," it says, "I hunger for the whole loaf of bread." We do not just seek the bits and pieces of righteousness; we hunger and thirst for all the righteousness there is, the whole thing. The construction of this text says to hunger and thirst for the entire loaf and the full pitcher. When you and I hunger and thirst for righteousness, we want the whole amount of righteousness available. We can never be satisfied until we get all the righteousness there is to get.

That is what people so seldom do. They are content with a part of righteousness. A man may have honesty and morality, and his respectability may be beyond question. But only he and God know if he is righteous in the eyes of God. We may be righteous on Sunday or around our Christian family and friends, but are we righteous on Thursday and when we are with friends and peers? We may pray, but do we also read and study our Bible? We may not lose our temper at church, but do we come unglued at home? Partial righteousness is unacceptable to God, and this passage teaches the opposite.

The Result of a Starving Spirit:

They shall be filled (satisfied). "Filled" is a great word. We use it to describe foddering an animal. It means to be satisfied. God wants to make us happy and satisfied. But satisfied with what? For what are we hungry and thirsty? Righteousness.

Notice the paradox! We are satisfied but never satisfied. My wife makes a delicious Polish dish called Perogies. I am always so satisfied when I eat that meal, but I always want more. I'm full, but I always want more because what I have eaten makes me want more. So it is with righteousness. It fills us and the filling is so sweet, rich, and pleasant that we want more.

When we seek God's righteousness, He grants it:

> Psalm 107: 9 – *He has satisfied the thirsty soul, and the hungry soul He has filled with what is good ....*

> Psalm 34:10 – *But they who seek the LORD shall not be in want of any good thing.*

> Psalm 23 – *I shall not want,* and *my cup overflows.*

> Jeremiah 31:14 – *My people shall be satisfied with My goodness, declares the LORD.*

> John 4:14 – Jesus told the woman at the well, *Whoever drinks of the water that I shall give him shall never thirst.*

> John 6:35 – *I am the bread of life, he who comes to Me shall not hunger.*

Jesus satisfies, yet there is a blessed dissatisfaction that wants even more and will be satisfied only when we see Jesus Christ. A kingdom person has a consuming ambition, not for power or pleasure, possessions, or praise, but for righteousness.

Marks of a Starving Spirit:

- **Am I satisfied with myself?** The Puritans used to say, "He has the most need of righteousness who least wants it." Or am I self-righteous and think everybody else is wrong and I am right? I am not hungry or thirsting after God's righteousness if I have any sense of self-satisfaction.

- **Does anything external satisfy me?** Do things influence how I feel? Do I fill my appetite with the wrong stuff and then lose that appetite? A hunger for righteousness will be satisfied with nothing else.

- **Do I have a great appetite for the Word of God?** Righteousness and sanctification come from the Word of God (John 17:17). Jeremiah 15:16 says, *Thy words were found and I ate them!* So, therefore, I am hungry and thirsty for righteousness, I will devour the Word of God because that is how I become righteous.

- **Do I love the things of God?** Proverbs 27:7 says, *To a famished man any bitter things are sweet.* Can I recognize someone who is seeking righteousness? When God brings devastation into their life, they are filled and satisfied. They receive it from God, even though it is painful. Some people can rejoice only when good things happen.

- **Is my hunger and thirst unconditional?** Remember the rich young ruler who told Jesus he wanted to know how to enter the kingdom but wasn't willing to give up his possessions? His hunger was conditional, and he never received that filling. What about me? Do I say, "I want Christ and my sin? Christ and my pride? Christ and my illicit relationship? Christ and my cheating? Christ and my lying? Christ and my covetousness? Christ and my materialism?

A hungry man does not want food and a new suit. A thirsty man does not want water and a new pair of shoes. They just want food and water. Psalm 119:20 says, *My soul is crushed with longing after Your ordinances at all times.*

Review and Resolve:

1. What is the significance of the words "hunger" and "thirst?"
2. What two things does righteousness point to?
3. What does it mean to gain righteousness in bits and pieces?
4. Explain the "Paradox" noted in this lesson.
5. Give the "Marks of a Starving Spirit."
6. Resolve to do one thing this week to give you a greater hunger.

Chapter 6

The Compassion Given to the Merciful

Blessed are the merciful, for they shall receive mercy.
(Matthew 5:7)

A Pastor called on one of the members of his church and found the man in the field plowing new ground with a yellow mule. As the pastor approached, he was surprised to hear the man swearing. The pastor told his parishioner that it was sinful to swear. The man responded: "See here, preacher, I have been a Christian for only a year. I broke this mule with cursing, and he won't go without it. I don't call it cursing, I call it driving the mule."

It seems to be the artificial adaptation of religion. The emphasis on the external rather than the internal is one of our age's great sins. But unfortunately, It was also the great sin of Jesus' day.

Jesus Confronts the External:

The religion Jesus faced in His day was shallow, superficial, external, and ritualistic. The Jewish leaders thought they were secure, and that God would include them in His kingdom. They thought they would be leaders in Messiah's rule. But Jesus thought differently. Of them, he said: *For you are like whitewashed tombs which on the outside appear beautiful, but inside they are full of dead men's bones and all uncleanness* (Matthew 23:27). They didn't fool John the Baptist either. When the Pharisees and Sadducees came to him for baptism, he said: *You brood of vipers, who warned you to flee from the wrath to come? Therefore, bring forth fruit in keeping with your repentance; and do not suppose that you can say to yourselves, 'We have Abraham for our father'* (Matthew 3:7-9). In other words, don't count on your racial identity to save you.

Jesus confronts this external, self-righteous, selfish crowd by telling them, "What matters is on the inside." He bypassed all the supposed credits they had given to themselves and went straight to the heart of the matter. Christ always emphasizes the inside. He is not unconcerned with outward action, but only as proper motivation produces it.

Righteousness on the inside will produce the fruit of right action. But we can falsify action without reality, and that is legalism. What Jesus wants is action that springs from right character.

Matthew's sixth and seventh chapters deal with action: things we do, say, or think. The heart attitude is the premise on which the whole Sermon builds. Martyn Lloyd Jones said, "A Christian *is* something before he *does* something!"

To be a child of the King, a subject of the Kingdom, is first to possess a certain kind of character, a character of brokenness, mourning over sin, meekness, a hunger and thirst for righteousness, mercifulness, purity of heart, a peacemaking quality. God never meant for us to control our Christianity, but for our Christianity to control us!

The Beatitudes and Action:

The first four Beatitudes are inner principles, dealing with how we see ourselves before God. This fifth Beatitude, while also being an inner attitude, begins to reach out to touch others. This Beatitude is the fruit of the other four. The first four are the **BE**atitudes, and the last four are the **DO**atitudes. So, when we are broken beggars in our spirit, mournful and meek and hungering and thirsting after righteousness, being merciful to others will be the result.

Notice that the first four Beatitudes line up with the last four. The first four are inner attitudes and the last four are things the attitudes manifest. So, for example, when we have poverty of spirit and realize we are nothing but beggars, we will be merciful and willing to give to another beggar. When we mourn over sin, we wash our hearts pure with the tears of penitence, and we will be pure in heart. When we are gentile or meek, we will be peacemakers because gentleness makes peace. And when we are hungering and thirsting for righteousness, we will be willing to be persecuted for righteousness' sake.

What Mercy IS NOT:

What does it mean to be merciful? The Jews of that day hardly knew. They were as merciless as the Romans. They were proud, egotistical, self-righteous, and condemning. What Jesus was saying touched them where they lived.

People often want to take this Beatitude in a humanistic way. They say, "Well if you are good to everybody else, everybody else will be good to you." Even the Talmud quotes Gamaliel as saying, "Whenever you have mercy, God will have mercy on you, and if you have not mercy, neither will God have mercy on you." It seems built into human thinking that if you are good to everybody, they will return the kindness. Even Gamaliel thought, "If I do this for God, God's going to do that for me."

One writer paraphrased this Beatitude: "This is the great truth of life; if people see us care, they will care." William Barclay translates verse 7 as follows: "O the bliss of the man who gets right inside other people until he can see with their eyes, think with their thoughts, feel with their feelings, for he who does that will find others do the same for him, and will know that is what God in Jesus Christ has done!"

However, it is not that simple. The world does not work that way! The Roman world did not know the meaning of mercy, no matter what good they did. A Roman philosopher said mercy was "the disease of the soul," a sign of weakness. The Romans glorified justice, courage, discipline, and power; they looked down on mercy. When a child was born into the Roman world, the father held his thumb up if he wanted the child and held it down if he didn't. If he held his thumb down, the servant immediately drowned the child.

Mercy and Grace:

What about mercy and grace? The term mercy and all its derivatives always presuppose problems. It deals with pain, misery, and distress. But grace deals with sin itself. Mercy deals with the symptoms, grace deals with the problems. Mercy offers relief from punishment; grace offers pardon for the crime. First comes grace. Grace removes sin. Then comes mercy, which eliminates the punishment. Grace is God giving me what I do not deserve. Mercy is when God does not give me what I do deserve.

When we talk about God's mercy, we do not speak of foolish sentimentality excusing sin. The only time God ever extended mercy was when somebody else paid the price for the sin involved. God never violates the truth of His justice and holiness for mercy. He will be merciful, but only after He carries out justice.

There will be merciless judgment on people who do not accept the truth of the sacrifice of Christ. We are not talking about sentimentality. If we sin our lives away and never acknowledge Jesus Christ, God offers no promise of mercy or acceptance but judgment without mercy.

Mercy Reaches Out:

Mercy is special. It is more than forgiveness. It is less than love. It is different from grace, and it is one with justice. The merciful not only hear the insults of evil men, but also reaches out to them in compassion. The merciful one is sympathetic, forgiving, gracious, and loving. He is not so sentimental that he will allow sin to go unpunished or unconfronted just because somebody is sad or tragic.

Psalm 37:21 (KJV) says: *The wicked borrow and do not pay it back again: but the righteous shows mercy.* If my son comes to me and says: "Dad, I did something wrong, and I am sorry," I'll be merciful. But I told my children since they were little, "If I find out you have not told me the truth and haven't admitted something you've done, there will be no mercy. There will be punishment. There will be 'trouble in the village.'"

Abraham's mercy after his nephew Lot wronged him caused him to secure Lot's deliverance. It was mercy in Joseph after mistreatment by his brothers that caused him to accept them and meet their needs. It was mercy in Moses after Miriam rebelled against him, and the Lord gave her leprosy, that made him cry, *Oh God, heal her, I pray!* (Numbers 12:13). It was mercy in David that twice caused him to spare the life of Saul.

The merciful are those who reach out, not those who grasp and take. God helps us somehow to overrule the inundation of a corrupt society and hear the voice of our God, who tells us to give everything we have. If somebody offends us, we should be merciful. Be compassionate. Be benevolent. Be sympathetic. If somebody makes a mistake or a misjudgment or fails to pay a debt or return something borrowed, be merciful. We must live the character of the kingdom.

Proverbs 11:17 says, *The merciful man does himself good, but the cruel man does himself harm.* Do you want misery? Be merciless! The reverse is true. If you want to read the characteristics of a godless society, read Romans 1:29-31. Notice the last one is *unmerciful.*

The Source of Mercy:

God is the source of mercy, but only for those moving through the four preceding Beatitudes. We must change inwardly and live the life of the kingdom before enjoying kingdom benefits. People want the blessing, but not the belonging. They are like Balaam, the false prophet, who said, *Let me die the death of the upright!* (Numbers 23:10). A Puritan commentator said, "Balaam wanted to die like the righteous all right, he just didn't want to live like the righteous." Therefore, the only people who receive mercy are those who come broken and beggarly before a holy God to seek His righteousness.

The Substance of Mercy:

What does it mean to be merciful? Matthew 5-6, Romans 15, II Corinthians 1, Galatians 6, Ephesians 4, and Colossians 3, along with countless other passages, will all answer this question for you, for they call us to be merciful. How can we be merciful?

- **Physically.** Giving a poor man money, a hungry man food, naked man clothes, and a bedless man a bed. Mercy never holds a grudge, retaliates, takes vengeance, flaunts somebody's weakness, makes something of someone's failure, or recites a sin. St. Augustine was so merciful that he invited people with no place to eat to his big, beautiful dining room table. He had engraved on the top of the table: "Whoever loves another's name to blast, this table's not for him. So let him fast." St. Grace

Sterling (a dear old saint from Gateway Baptist Church now with her Lord) invited hungry people to eat at her table and homeless people to live in her home.

- **Spiritually.** Augustine said, "If I weep for the body from which the soul is departed, should I not weep for the soul from which God is departed?" We cry a lot of tears over dead bodies. What do we do when it comes to souls?

I hear Stephen saying as they cast the stones that crushed out his life, *Lord, do not hold this sin against them!* (Acts 7:60). He was pitying their souls. You and I must look at the lost with pity, not lording it over them or thinking ourselves better.

The Sequel to Mercy:

The sequel to mercy is obtaining mercy. What a beautiful thing. Do you see the cycle? God gives us mercy, we are merciful, and God gives us more mercy. II Samuel 22:26 says the same thing that it is the merciful who receive mercy. James 2:13 says negatively, *For judgment will be merciless to one who has shown no mercy.* It's there in Psalm 18 and Proverbs 14, as well.

However, some people think being merciful is how we get saved. This error of the Roman Catholic Church says God is satisfied and gives mercy when we do merciful deeds. That view spawned monasteries and nunneries, and everything related to them. But this is not the way to earn salvation. We cannot get mercy for merit. Mercy can apply only where there is no merit, or it is not mercy.

Review and Resolve:

1. How did the Jews practice an external religion?
2. What is the relationship of the first four Beatitudes to the last four Beatitudes?
3. What do we say in this lesson that Mercy is **NOT**?
4. So, define what Mercy **IS**.
5. What is the difference between Mercy and Grace?
6. Define the two ways that you and I can be merciful.
7. What will you resolve to do this week to be merciful?

Chapter 7

The Comprehension of the Pure in Heart

Blessed are the pure in heart, for they shall see God.
(Matthew 5:8)

*L*udwig Richter, the great German painter, used to relate with considerable emotion that his mother repeatedly told him to repeat the Beatitudes when he met temptation. But she also told him that when he came to *Blessed are the Pure in Heart,* he should repeat it seven times. "How often," says Richter in his autobiography, "have I felt the power of these holy words, especially when I remember that in my distant home mother was, perhaps in the hour of my temptation, raising her voice in intercession for her son."

The same man wrote in the space under his portrait Goethe's words: "Great thoughts and a pure heart, these we should ask of God."

An Incredible Statement:

Blessed are the pure in heart, for they shall see God" Sometimes we come to a statement in Scripture that we don't feel we can handle, let alone grip and transmit it to others. It seems it is a bottomless pit with immeasurable depths. Attempting.to deal with this Beatitude in one brief lesson almost insults God and the power, depth, and insight of His wonderful Word. This Beatitude stretches over everything else revealed in Scripture. The theme of purity of heart is necessary to see God is vast and infinite drawing in almost every Biblical thread.

There is no way to uncover all that is in these words, but I have asked the Lord to enable me to at least focus on a rich and meaningful central lesson. Then with His help, we may see the depth of this statement.

The Cultural Context:

We already discussed the political situation in Israel. However, it is also essential we understand the spiritual condition of Israel at the time Jesus made this statement. An oppressive authoritative character on the part of the Pharisees burdened Israel. They were the dominant influence and force in Israel at the time. A legalistic system draws such absolute boundaries around what is spiritually acceptable that, by its definitive character, it tends to oppress and reign wherever it exists.

The Pharisees had misinterpreted the Law of Moses they pacified their consciences by maintaining traditions if they could not keep God's laws. So, they formed a relentless and rigid legalistic system, which was impossible to perform. The leaders decided that if one could keep just a few laws, God would understand. Then they couldn't even do that, so they agreed God would understand if a person could find one law and keep it. Hence the question of the lawyer in Matthew 22:36: *Teacher, what is the great commandment in the law?*

The people were crying for a savior, a redeemer, who would not impose more rules but forgive them for the ones they had always broken. They knew the word of Ezekiel that someday, God would come and cleanse them. They knew that David said, *How blessed is the man to whom the LORD does not impute iniquity* (Psalm 32:2). So when John the Baptist came preaching,

Repent for the kingdom of heaven is at hand, (Matthew 32:2) they could not get there fast enough.

Nicodemus is a good example. He was a Pharisee and a pretty honest man (I believe his integrity drew him to Christ). In the Greek of John 3:1, an emphatic is used to describe him. This man was *the* teacher, *the* ruler of the Jews, the top man in terms of recitation of divine principles. But his heart was anxious, and he had great insight into who Jesus really was.

In John 6, Jesus fed the 5,000. They said, *What shall we do, that we may work the works of God?* Jesus answered, *This is the work of God, that you believe in Him whom He has sent* (John 6:28-29).

They were saying the same thing as Nicodemus. "We know the whole legal system. We know the ritualistic routine. We have got all the ceremonies down. But it does not satisfy us spiritually, and we want to know the reality of the work of God." They wanted something real. They wanted to know how you get into the kingdom because they realized nobody would get there by keeping the law.

A lawyer asked the same question of Jesus in Luke 10:25: *Behold a certain lawyer stood up and put Him to the test, saying, 'Teacher, what shall I do to inherit eternal life?'* It is the same question as that of the 5,000 and Nicodemus. "What is the standard?" How do you get relief from guilt, anxiety, and frustration when faced with a legal system to please God, and you know you cannot keep it?

That is the question Jesus answers in the Beatitudes. And more than any other single Beatitude, 5:8 answers. *Blessed are the pure in heart, for they (they and they alone) shall see God.* It is not those who observe the external washings, go through the ceremonies, or practice the religion of human achievement.

God's Standard:

When God set a standard for acceptable behavior, He did not say you had to be better than a Publican or an immoral man. He said, "If you want to see God, you must be pure." In the sermon itself, in Matthew 5:48, Jesus said, *Therefore you are to be perfect, as your heavenly Father is perfect.* That is the standard of the absolute, sovereign, righteous, and holy God of the universe. The Pharisees got uptight without certain washings of the hands, pots, and pans. They were great for tithing mint, cumin, and dill. So, they gave ten percent of some tiny herb leaf, but paid no attention to love, truth, and mercy. So, Jesus told them, *For you are like whitewashed tombs which on the outside appear beautiful, but inside they are full of dead men's bones and all uncleanness* (Matthew 23:27). The Lord sheds that whole cloak of hypocrisy in one statement.

The Context of the Beatitudes:

Please take note that all the Beatitudes are equally important. They are all part of the same great reality. Realize the kingdom person fulfills all these descriptions. We cannot pick and choose. The first seven Beatitudes fit a beautiful pattern. The first three lead up to the fourth, which seems to be the apex. Then these last three Beatitudes flow out of the fourth, after the first three lead up to it.

But there is something even more intricate. The first and the fifth, the second and the sixth, and the third and the seventh seem to fit together. The poor in spirit (first) who realize they are nothing but beggars who will reach out in mercy to others (fifth). Those who mourn over sin (second) will know the purity of heart (sixth). Finally, there are the meek (third) who are the peacemakers (seventh). The beautiful weaving of these Beatitudes shows how the mind of God works. This one is in the right place historically and chronologically.

How the Beatitudes Fit Together:

1. Blessed are the poor in spirit	5. Blessed are the merciful
2. Blessed are those who mourn	6. Blessed are the pure in heart
3. Blessed are the gentle	7. Blessed are the peacemakers
4. Blessed are those who hunger and thirst after righteousness.	8. Blessed are those who are persecuted

Two Kinds of Religion:

There are only two kinds of religion in the world. One is of human achievement, which comes under every brand imaginable but is all from the same base: you earn your way. The other is of divine accomplishment saying, "I can't do it. God did it for me in Christ."

Take your pick! Human achievement is Satan's lie. In every crowd, you have people who will make it on their own; they will try to earn their way to heaven and get there on their own energy, power, and resources. That day, they were in that crowd, and the Lord Jesus stripped them bare. "Sorry folks. You don't qualify to see God. You will never be in My Kingdom because it is for the 'Pure in Heart.'"

Pure in Heart:

In the Bible, we always see the heart as the inside of man, the seat of his personality. Predominantly, it refers to the thinking process. The heart is not specifically the emotions. The Bible speaks of emotions, as the *bowels of compassion"* or the feeling in the stomach.

The mind and heart work together. *As a man thinks in his heart, so is he.* (Proverbs 23:7). Sometimes the word "heart" does not refer to the will and emotion spinning from the intellect. For example, if my mind commits to something, it affects my will, which affects my emotions.

Proverbs 4:23 pulls all this together: *Watch over your heart with all diligence for from it flows the springs of life.* In other words, whatever the heart is, it is the source of life. The issues of thinking, feeling, and acting all spawn out of this heart.

When the Lord speaks of the "pure in heart, He thinks first of the mind, which controls the will and emotions. This phrase was a direct shot at the Pharisees and the legalists who told everyone to take care of the outside. Jesus was coming right at them. If you go to church every day of the week, carry a Bible, and recite verses, but your heart is not clean, you have not met God's standard.

But what does it mean to be pure? The Greek word Jesus uses here is "katharos," and points to "cleanse from filth and iniquity." It means to be free from sin and the word from which we receive our English word, "catharsis." Medical people know that a "cathartic" is an agent used to cleanse a wound or infected area to make it pure. So, when someone goes to a psychologist or a counselor, and they have a "catharsis," they have a soul cleansing.

Some suggest pure means "unmixed, unalloyed, unadulterated, sifted, or cleansed of chaff." In other words, pure means there is no added mixture of any foreign element. Thus, our Lord says, "I desire a heart unmixed in its devotion and motivation." Pure motives from a pure heart. This desire concerns attitudes, integrity, and singleness of heart instead of duplicity and double mindedness. Jeremiah 32:39 says, *And I will give them one heart and one way, that they may fear Me always.*

Jesus emphasizes that principle, as we shall see later in this Sermon, in chapter 6, *Where your treasure is, there will your heart be also* (6:21). He sums it all up in verse 24 when He says: *No one can serve two masters.* James discussed it in his epistle: *Cleanse your hands, you sinners; and purify your hearts, you double-minded"* (James 4:8).

Pure motive does not stop short of pure deeds. The word "katharos" goes beyond motive. Many people with pure motives never come to God. *Who can say, 'I have cleansed my heart, I am pure from my sin?'* Obviously, the answer is *nobody*!

Acts 15:9 says faith cleanses our hearts. We cannot do it by good works, but by believing. In what? 1 John 1:7 gives the answer: *If we walk in the light as He Himself is in the light, we have fellowship with one another, and the blood of Jesus Christ His Son cleanses us from all sin.* In Mexico City, people at the Shrine of Guadalupe crawl on their knees for three hundred yards until bleeding. Very sincere, but very wrong. No doubt the worshipers of Baal in Elijah's day had sincerity when they took their knives and hacked themselves. I'd say that is sincerity! When you cut yourself up, you mean business. But there's more than that in the word "katharos." It is not just a pure motive, but a holy deed (as defined by God). Both must be there.

How do You Acquire a Pure Heart?

Know you cannot do it by yourself. That is the first step. Proverbs 20:9 asks, "Faith in what?" In the blood of Jesus Christ, which cleanses us from all sin. Do you want to be pure in heart? Accept the sacrifice of Christ on the cross!

If you are already a Christian, purify your heart through the words of Jesus and prayer. John 15:3 says, *You are already clean because of the word."* Stay in the word (Bible) and pray. Hear the words of Job, who said, *"Who can make the clean out of the unclean?* (14:4). Only one answer echoes down through eternity: "God can!"

The Wonderful Promise:

They shall see God. This phrase is a a future continuous tense in Greek. In other words, *They shall be continually seeing God for themselves.* Do you know what happens when God purifies our hearts at salvation? We live in the presence of God. We comprehend Him, realize He is there, and see Him with spiritual eyes. Like Moses, who cried, *I pray, show me Your glory"* (Exodus 33:18), the one whose heart Jesus Christ purifies sees the glory of God again and again. To see God was the most significant thing a person in the Old Testament could dream. Purity of heart cleanses the eyes of the soul so that God is visible.

Do you want to see God? Do you want God alive in your world, now and forever? Purify your heart. Some day you will see God with your physical eyes (I John 3:2). Oh, what a day to see Christ face to face!

Review and Resolve:

1. Why or how is the cultural context significant to this Beatitude?
2. What question does Jesus answer with this Beatitude?
3. What is the difference between God's standard and the Pharisees?
4. What does the arrangement of these Beatitudes tell us about God?
5. What are the two kinds of religion?
6. How can you become "Pure in Heart?"
7. What is most important about *"They shall see God?"*
8. How can you be **"Pure in Heart"** this week?

Chapter 8

The Calling of Peacemakers

Blessed are the peacemakers, for they shall be called sons of God. (Matthew 5:9)

November 27, 1995, marked the 100th anniversary of Alfred Bernard Nobel's last will and testament. Why is the date of a will commemorated? In his will, Nobel left the bulk of a vast fortune from the invention of dynamite and other explosives to the establishment of the "Nobel Peace Prize."

In 1867 at age thirty-four, Nobel was granted a patent for dynamite, and over the next twenty-nine years of his life, he became fabulously wealthy from the manufacture of explosives.

His will, dated November 27, 1895, provided for a trust to establish five prizes in peace, physics, chemistry, medicine, and literature. The recipients of the prizes were to receive a gold medal, a citation diploma, and cash awards of $30,000 to $40,000. Nobel added a sixth award in economic science in 1969.

Man has made many attempts at peace and the emphasis on peace. However, true peace only comes from God and the Bible. The idea of peace dominates the Bible. It began with the Garden of Eden and closes with peace forever in eternity. You could chart all Biblical history by the peace theme. There are 400 references to peace in the Bible and God Himself is the *God of peace.*

However, there is no peace in the world. And there are two reasons for this: [1] The opposition of Satan and [2] The disobedience of men. The fall of some angels and the fall of man has caused a world without peace.

Now we come to the seventh Beatitude, and it seems God is telling us we can have some influence in restoring the conditions that existed before the fall. We are to restore the world to the peace forfeited by our sinning. A special people whom He calls peacemakers are His agents in the world, and they are here to go far beyond anyone who wins the Nobel Peace Prize because the peace they offer is eternal, divine, and genuine.

The world's pacemakers have a terrible record. The peace we hail today begins to collapse tomorrow. We do not have political, economic, social, or domestic peace. We have peace nowhere because we have no peace in our hearts. That is the real issue! Someone has said, "Washington has lots of peace monuments. They build one after every war!"

Peace is merely that brief glorious moment in history when everybody stops to reload. Only eight percent of the time since the beginning of recorded history has the world been entirely at peace. In over 3,100 years, only 286 have been warless, with 8,000 treaties broken in that time. In the aftermath of World War II, the world was concerned with developing an agency for world peace, so in 1945 the United Nations brought itself into existence with the motto: "To have succeeding generations free from the scourge of war." Since then, there has not been one day of peace. Not one! It's a pipe dream, and now we all know there is no peace inside the United Nations.

There is no peace! We cannot get along. Every relationship is fragile. People deal with mental and emotional illness as never before. We see families break up, disorder, school shootings, fights between brothers and sisters, angry splits in churches, and wars among nations. There seems no end to it. Man has no peace in himself, so his world, which is merely a projection of himself, is riddled with chaos.

We want to understand what Christ means in Matthew 5:9, so we will look at five truths about peace.

The Meaning of Peace:

The Greek word for peace is "eirene," and the Hebrew word is "shalom." In both cases, the word goes beyond the negative state. Peace does not mean only the absence of trouble. Instead, it means "everything which makes for a man's highest good." In the east, when one man says to another, "Salaam," which is the same word as "shalom," he does not mean that he wishes only the absence of evil things. He wishes for him the presence of all good things. In the Bible, peace means freedom from all trouble and enjoyment of all good.

When a Jew says "Shalom," he does not merely mean, "May you have no war." Instead, he suggests, "May you have all the righteousness and goodness God can give."

There is a big difference between a truce and peace. A truce says you don't shoot for a while. Peace comes when the truth is known, which settles the issue, and the parties embrace each other. Stopping war is not real peace. Approaching peace that way may develop a far worse situation.

The peace of the Bible, however, never evades issues. It is not peace at any price. It is not glossing over. Instead, the peace of the Bible conquers the problem. It builds a bridge. Sometimes it means to struggle, sometimes, it means pain, and sometimes it means anguish, but real peace can come in the end. Biblically peace is real peace. *But the wisdom from above is first pure, then peaceable* (James 3:17). God's peace never comes at the expense of righteousness! *Pursue peace with all men, and the sanctification without which no one will see the Lord* (Hebrews 12:14). You cannot divorce peace from purity.

A true Biblical peacemaker will not let sleeping dogs lie. He will not save the status quo. He does not say, "I know the person's doing wrong, but I would rather have a peaceful situation. I want to keep the peace." That is a cop-out. Jesus was the greatest peacemaker, but He did not avoid conflict. They killed Him! So the meaning of peace is resolving conflict by the truth, as you bring to bear the righteousness and purity of God.

The Menace of Peace:

So, what is it that hinders peace? If the meaning of peace is righteousness and truth, then the menace of peace is error and lies. Further, we have entered a "post-truth" period in human history. Jeremiah 17:9 says, *The heart is more deceitful then all else and is desperately wicked.* We must understand that truth. How does a wicked heart manifest itself? Isaiah 48:22 says, *"There is no peace for the wicked, says the LORD."* Jeremiah says man's heart is deceitful, and because of that, Isaiah says he shall have no peace.

What we must face, then is a man with a defiled heart from which evil proceeds. That kind of person cannot produce peace because peace results from holiness and righteousness. James 3:18 says, *The seed whose fruit is righteousness is sown in peace by those who make peace.* Therefore, peacemakers sow righteous fruit.

If two people are fighting, it is always because of sin. *Always!* Eliminate the sin, and the fight is over. The only peacemakers on earth bring men to righteousness, to God's standards. Anyone can be a peacemaker if he follows the first six Beatitudes.

You will have peace if you have righteousness, purity, and holiness in your life. And if you have righteousness, purity, and holiness in your marriage, home, and nation, peace will be there, too, because that is always the way. Once you have righteousness, you are at peace with God, man, and yourself.

We are a society of people fighting for our rights and exalting ourselves. No wonder the Jews did not like Jesus. They wanted a fighter. When Jesus said, *Blessed are the peacemakers,* I'm sure they rolled their eyes. So today, people may look down on Christians and think of them as cowardly and weak. However, the only people who can have peace are the Christians.

The Maker of Peace:

Who is the maker of peace? Paul told us in I Corinthians 14:33: *For God is not a God of confusion but of peace.* God is the author, the maker, and the source of peace. Apart from Him, there is no peace. Several times the New Testament calls God the *God of Peace.*

II Thessalonians 3:16 says Jesus is the *"Lord of Peace."*

John MacArthur tells about a couple arguing back and forth in a divorce hearing. Their four-year-old boy was teary-eyed watching the conflict. Then he took his father's hand and his mother's hand and kept pulling until he pulled the two hands together. He became a peacemaker. That is what Christ did for us. He provided the righteousness that allows man to take the hand of God. Colossians 1:20 says that Jesus was able *to reconcile all things to Himself, having made peace through the blood of His cross.* The cross made peace where there was no peace, and there could be none in any other way.

So, God is the source of peace; Jesus is the manifestation of peace, and the Holy Spirit is the agency of peace. Galatians 5:22 tells us, *The fruit of the Spirit is love, joy, PEACE.*

Jesus said, *These things I have spoken to you that in Me you may have peace. In the world you have tribulation but take courage; I have overcome the world* (John 16:23). We Christians can abide in the Lord; and peace is there. No matter how much anxiety and turmoil there is in the world, there is a cushion of peace, an eye in the storm, in the soul of the person who knows the Prince of Peace, the one who has the indwelling Spirit of peace, given by the God of peace.

The Messengers of Peace:

We, the Christians, are the messengers of peace. I Corinthians 7:15 says, *God has called us to peace.* So, II Corinthians tells us, *Now all these things are from God, who reconciled us to Himself through Christ, and gave us the ministry of reconciliation* (peacemaking), *namely, that God was in Christ reconciling the world to Himself, not counting their trespasses against them, and He has committed to us the word of reconciliation. Therefore, we are ambassadors for Christ, as though God were entreating through us; we beg you on behalf of Christ, be reconciled to God.* We are God's peace corps in the truest sense of the word. Other Scriptures discuss this: Colossians 3:15, *Let the peace of Christ rule in your hearts.* Philippians 4:7, *The peace of God shall guard your hearts and your minds in Christ Jesus.*

You may ask, "As a peacemaker, what do I do?" Three things:

- **Make Peace With God Yourself!** Accept the Gospel of peace (Ephesians 6:15). God made peace with us in Christ and the cross. Every time there is sin in our lives, that peace is interrupted, and we cannot commune freely with God. Therefore, we must confess sin quickly to find peace between God and us. Someone might say, "Dear God, I shouldn't have said that thing to my wife this morning. Will you please forgive me for that? Thank you!" Then it would be a good idea to ask your wife to forgive you too.

- **Help Others Make Peace With God!** The greatest thing about peace-making is that we can go to someone at war with God and make peace between that person and God. The moment that person comes to Christ, he makes peace with God, and then he will be at peace with us. When he becomes a child of God, he becomes our brother.

- **Evangelism Is Peacemaking.** The best way to be a peacemaker is to preach the gospel of Jesus Christ. No wonder it says in Romans 10:15, *How beautiful are the feet of those who bring glad tidings of good things.* Do you want to be a peacemaker? Tell somebody about Jesus Christ.

- **Make Peace With Men!** Bring men together with each other. This task is not always easy, especially if you are the one who must make peace with someone else. God does not want people coming to church and worshiping Him if they know someone has something against them. Here is some Scripture:

  > *If therefore you are presenting your offering at the altar, and there remember that your brother has something against you, leave your offering there before the altar, and go your way; first be reconciled to your brother, and then come and present your offering* (Matthew 5:23-24).

Be at peace with one another (Mark 9:50). This command means between you and your spouse, brother, sister, neighbor, and fellow church member.

  > *If possible, so far as it depends on you, be at peace with all men* (Romans 12:18).

The Merit of Peace:

You might ask, what is the result of being a peacemaker? According to this Beatitude, you will be called a *Son of God.* I couldn't think of anything better for God to call us, could you? The Greek word which Jesus uses for "son" is a word that speaks of all the dignity, honor, and standing of a son. So, Christ is not merely talking about the affection that belongs to us. He is talking about dignity, honor, and the standing which comes from being God's son.

We are His sons. The Bible says we are the apple of His eye. We immediately think of some shiny little apple. But what the Hebrew language meant by the apple of the eye was the pupil, the most vulnerable part of the body. It's the tenderest part, the most sensitive part. You protect it. When anything comes toward your eye's pupil, you shield it.

God feels that way about His children. So, you touch one of His children, it means you poke your finger in His eye. He says in Malachi 3:17 that we are His jewels. Isaiah 56:5 says that He will give us an everlasting name. Psalm 56:8 says He keeps our tears in His bottle. Isn't that fabulous? When you cried over something, an old Hebrew custom was to store your tears in a bottle so people would know how you sorrowed. God keeps our tears in His bottle to treasure the evidence of our sorrow.

When we die, this truth becomes the most beautiful thing of all. Psalm 116:15 says, *Precious in the sight of the LORD is the death of His godly ones.* We matter to God. We are His sons. He makes us princes, kings, priests, and fellow heirs. In Psalm 16:3, He calls us the *majestic ones.* In II Timothy 2:21, a *vessel for honor.* Revelation says we shall get to sit with Him on His throne.

God makes you an heir to everything He possesses. God works everything for your good. He keeps you from perishing forever. And He gives you heaven. You can always tell such a son of God. He is a peacemaker.

Review and Resolve:

1. What do you think of the attempts of mankind to bring about peace in the world?
2. Explain what peace really is from a Biblical point of view.
3. When two people are fighting, what is always the cause?
4. How does the Trinity relate to peace as taught in our lesson?
5. What three things must you do to be a peacemaker?
6. What does being a "son of God" mean to you?

Chapter 9

The Condition of the Persecuted

Blessed are those who have been persecuted for the sake of righteousness, for theirs is the kingdom of heaven. Blessed are you when men revile you, and persecute you, and say all kinds of evil against you falsely, on account of Me. Rejoice, and be glad, for your reward in heaven is great, for so they persecuted the prophets who were before you.

The French reformer, Theodore Beza, made a famous retort to King Henry of Navarre: "Sire, it is truly the lot of the Church of God, for which I speak, to endure blows and not to strike them. But may it please you to remember that it is an anvil which has worn out many hammers."

This statement has proven true over the years of church history. One of the most famous instances of martyrdom worldwide occurred in Smyrna in A.D. 155. An edict had been given that all were to worship Caesar. Polycarp, who was led to Jesus Christ by the Apostle Paul, was the leader, perhaps the pastor, of the church in Smyrna (His tomb remains there to this day). Polycarp was arrested at a friend's home outside the city and taken before Iren arch Herod, who asked, "What harm is there in saying Caesar is Lord, or in participating in these ceremonies so that you can be spared."

Polycarp answered, "I cannot do as you advise me; I cannot say 'Caesar is Lord.' I can only say 'Jesus is Lord.'"

The pagan leader commanded his soldiers to give him to the lions and burn him at the stake. While in the arena, the proconsul said to him, "Swear by the fortune of Caesar, and I will set you free; reproach Christ, and I will stop all this."

Polycarp answered with one of the most famous avowals in all history: "Eighty and six years have I served Him, and He never did me any injury. How can I blaspheme my King and Savior?" When the proconsul again pressed him, the aged pastor said, "Since you are vainly urging that I should swear by the fortune of Caesar and pretend not to know who and what I am, hear me now, I am a Christian!"

A little later, the governor threatened, "I have wild beasts at hand; to these will I cast you, except you change your mind."

Polycarp replied: "You threaten me with fire, which burns for an hour, and after a little while is extinguished, but you are ignorant of the fire of the coming judgment and the eternal punishment reserved for the ungodly. But why do you wait? Do what you will to me!"

Soon afterward, the people, led by the Jews, gathered the wood and burned the faithful pastor. But in flames, this prayer was recorded: "I thank thee that thou hast graciously thought me worthy of this day and of this hour that I may receive a portion in the number of Thy martyrs in the cup of Thy Christ."

The Eighth Beatitude:

We come to the eighth Beatitude, which deals with persecution. This persecution is general in verse 10, *Blessed are those....* However, when we come to verse 11, the whole thing becomes more personal, *Blessed are you....* Although persecution repeats in slightly different terms in these verses, it is all one Beatitude. Verse 10 speaks of persecution in general, and verse 11 expands and personalizes the concept. Finally, in verse 12, the historical persecution of the prophets comes into view. The result is given at the end of verse 10, *Theirs is the kingdom of heaven* and in verse 12, *Your reward in heaven is great.*

We should note there is no change in character between the person practicing the 8th Beatitude and the previous Beatitude. Therefore, if a person is practicing the first 7 Beatitudes, he will not avoid the persecution of the 8th.

The Meaning of Persecution

The word which Jesus uses in these verses, and he uses it three times, means "to put to flight, drive away, to pursue, or to chase away." It finally came to mean "to harass or treat evilly." It is the attitude (as the other Beatitudes are also attitudes) of being willing to be persecuted. It is that lack of fear, that lack of shame, that presence of boldness that says, "I will be in this world what Christ would have me be. I will say in this world what Christ would have me say and if persecution results, let it be."

It is a passive participle in Greek, indicating the permissiveness of those who allow persecution of themselves. In other words, it is something done to them. "Blessed are those who allow persecution of themselves." And since it is a perfect participle, this persecution happens with continuing results. As a result of living a Beatitude life, the believer is constantly willing to accept whatever comes. At this point, some people bail out.

Persecution in the Bible:

- Paul says, *Persecutions, sufferings, such as happened to me at Antioch, at Iconium and at Lystra; what persecutions I endured, and out of them all the Lord delivered me! And indeed, all who desire to live godly lives in Christ Jesus will be persecuted* (II Timothy 3:11-12).

- *But as at that time, he who was born according to the flesh persecuted him who was born according to the Spirit, so it is now also* (Galatians 4:29).

- *For to you it has been granted for Christ's sake, not only to believe in Him, but also to suffer for His sake* (Philippians 1:29).

- *For indeed when we were with you, we kept telling you in advance that we were going to suffer affliction; and so, it came to pass, as you know* (I Thessalonians 3:4).

Inevitable Persecution

Persecution is part of being a Christian. It is ordained. Living in direct opposition to Satan in his world and system will inevitably bring antagonism and persecution from those who do not respond to our message. Christlikeness produces the same reaction as when Jesus Himself was on earth.

Thomas Watson, the Puritan writer, perceives this when he writes, "Though they be ever so meek, merciful, pure in heart, their piety will never shield them from suffering. They must hang their harp on the willows and take the cross. The way to heaven is by the way of thorns and blood. Set it down as a maxim, if you will follow Christ, you will see the swords and staves. Put the cross in your creed." We'd better examine our claim to be Christians if we don't have any persecution. If I am not causing flack in the world, if I am not making waves, if I am not generating some conflict, then maybe something is seriously wrong.

We have lived somewhat tolerant in North America regarding public or governmental persecution. That seems to have changed in recent years. But wherever you live a redeemed life to its hilt, wherever you live out the principles of the kingdom life, wherever you are an obedient son of God, living the righteousness of Christ in this world, it will come to be obnoxious to Satan. Always!

The Way of Escape:

Oh, we can escape! We can go through our whole lives without persecution. First, approve the world's standards. Fit right in. Accept the world's morals and ethics. Live as the world lives. Laugh at its jokes, enjoy its entertainment, and smile when it mocks God. Let it take His name in vain. Don't tell people they are sinners. Don't tell people they are lost without Jesus Christ, and don't tell people they are doomed to death, and whatever you do, don't mention hell!

I promise you; they will not persecute you. And if that is your choice, examine yourself to see whether you are actually in the faith. You may be a Christian living in disobedience, or you might not be a Christian at all. Just remember Luke 9:26, where Jesus says, *whoever is ashamed of Me and My words, of him will the Son of Man be ashamed.* It can happen. In Luke 6:26, our Lord says, *Woe to you when all men speak well of you.* Don't ever forget that when you are popular with everybody, it is because they do not know the truth about you. So, either you have masked your Christianity, or you are not a Christian at all.

Over 100 years ago, a man came to Tertullian and said, "I have come to Christ, but I don't know what to do. I have a job that I don't think is right, but I have to live."

To which Tertullian replied, "Must you?" Here is where the rubber of Christianity meets the road. Here is where you separate the men from the boys in Christianity. It could become the most significant commitment you will ever make. Our only choice is loyalty to Jesus Christ, even if we must die. The early Christians' loyalty to Christ greatly affected their social, political, and religious lives. When they became Christians, they wondered, "What do I do with my friends? Do I eat the meat offered to idols? Do I go to the pagan temple for the entertainment?" Or do I pay the price of separation? We still make similar choices in our world and culture.

They chose Christ. They refused to compromise. They became dissidents, rebels, pockets of disloyalty, and threats to the Empire's solidarity. One poet described them as "the panting, huddling flock whose only crime was Christ." They faced torture for their stand, and we must be willing to do the same.

The Type of Persecution:

Maybe our society tolerates Christianity because our standard is so low. We compromise all the time. Jesus adds to the list of Beatitudes the certainty of persecution. How are we to be persecuted? There are three ways in verse 11: "Reviled," "Persecuted," and "All kinds of evil." We have already dealt with the persecution idea. Let's look at the others.

Revile: This word in Greek means "cast in one's teeth." It was used at Christ's crucifixion Christ in Matthew 27:44 when they *mocked Him, (made fun), reviled Him, and scorned Him.* It is to throw something into one's face, to abuse with vile, vicious, and mocking words.

So, people will not only chase us out of the groups we used to be in, but we will also be subject to evil spoken of us. I have found that I could take away a little of the chasing. Nobody wants me around much after they discover I am a confronting and conservative minister; unlike other ministers they have known. I have usually been able to handle people saying unkind and vile things about me. I have taken a stand among the pagans and other so-called conservative Christians.

All Kinds of Evil:

However, when we come to the third one: *and say all kinds of evil against you falsely,* I become concerned. When they claim I say things I don't say, that's hard to take. Then I want to attempt to defend myself over something I never even said.

Christ's first standards were so high that the Jews must have fallen on their backs like toy soldiers. Then He added to the standards, "And by the way, if you want to live this way, you will be persecuted and chased out of your jobs, homes, and society."

People will speak violently and viciously against you and say things about you that aren't true."

Yes, "Rejoice!" The Greek word means to be extra glad. If that is not enough, He says, *be exceedingly glad,* which means to jump and skip and shout for joy. You say, "you've got to be out of your mind!" Perhaps. But two reasons exist why you should be happy about all this.

- Verse 12––*Your reward in heaven is great.* Heaven is how long? Forever! How long is "now"? A vapor that appears for an instant and then vanishes away (James 4:14). The word "great" means abundant. It is the fullness of reward. So, Paul says in II Timothy 4:8, *In the future there is laid up for me the crown of righteousness, which the Lord, the righteous Judge, will award to me on that day; and not only to me, but also to all who have loved His appearing.*

- Verse 12––*They persecuted the prophets also.* We are in pretty good company when people persecute us––an elite circle. Jesus is saying, "If you have any doubt about your salvation, if you question whether or not you are in the kingdom, the persecution from unbelievers will convince you beyond a shadow of a doubt that you belong to God, because they'll be doing to you exactly what they did to the prophets God called." Great truth! When persecution comes to me, I say, "Oh, I know I'm your child, Lord, and I know I stand in the ranks of the prophets!" The world does not persecute people who are not the prophets of God and who don't speak the message of God.

Persecution is a verification that you belong to a righteous line. Here is the believer's security. Here is the climax of the Beatitudes. Jesus offers salvation and tells us how to know we have it. It does not come from some theological prescription. It does not come from knowing we decided way back when. Our security comes from knowing we live a confrontive life in an ungodly world that persecutes us for righteousness' sake.

Conclusion:

John Knox, the Scottish preacher, was paid this great tribute: "He feared God so much that he never dared to fear any man."

Chrysostom, a renowned Christian of ancient times, was summoned before the Roman Emperor Arcadius and threatened with banishment if he didn't cease to proclaim Jesus. He replied, "Sire, you cannot banish me, for the world is my Father's house."

"Then I'll slay you!" exclaimed the angered ruler.

"Nay, but you cannot, for my life is hid with Christ in God."

"Your treasures will be confiscated!" came the fiery retort.

"Sire, that cannot be. My treasures are in heaven, where none can break through and steal."

"But I will drive you from man, and you will have no friends left!"

"That you cannot do either, for I have a friend in heaven who has said, 'I will never leave you nor forsake you.'"

Ultimately, the Emperor banished him to the edge of Armenia. Still, he continued to influence his friends with letters, until his enemies determined to oust him farther away, but he died on the journey.

What about us? What are our priorities? What do we say to ourselves? What rings true about us in our minds, in our hearts? Do we understand what the Beatitudes are saying? It isn't the rich or proud. It isn't the frivolous, the fierce, the full, the cunning, the warlike, or the favorites of the earthly kings who enter the kingdom. Instead, it is the poor, the meek, the sorrowing, the hungry, the sincere, the peacemakers, and the persecuted. They enter, and the proof of their citizenship is that the world hates them. Ironic!

Review and Resolve:

1. What does the "passive participle" indicate about this concept of being persecuted?
2. Why do you think our modern world tolerates Christianity so easily?
3. Why is loyalty to Christ the only choice we have?
4. Name and define the three types of persecution.
5. What should be our response to persecution, and how on earth do we do it?
6. What are the two reasons we should have such a response?
7. Can you write when and how you became a Christian?

Chapter 10

Do We Make Men Thirsty?

You are the salt of the earth; but if the salt has become taste-less, how will it be made salty again? It is good for nothing any more, except to be thrown out and trampled underfoot by men. You are the light of the world. A city set on a hill cannot be hidden. Nor do men light a lamp, and put it under the peck-measure, but on the lampstand; and it gives light to all who are in the house. Let your light shine before men in such a way that they may see your good works, and glorify your Father who is in heaven (Matthew 5:13-16).

Daniel Webster's testimony to his belief in Jesus Christ may be seen and read by anyone who cares to visit Marshfield, Mass., and the burial place of the great statesman. He lies buried half a mile back from his house, by the side of his wife and three children. His rough granite tomb is entirely unpretentious, with a sod roof.

Webster dictated his epitaph the day before his death. It is as follows:

Daniel Webster,
Born January 18, 1782,
Died October 24:1854

> *Philosophical argument, especially that drawn from the vast-*
> *ness, in comparison with the apparent insignificance of this*
> *globe, had sometimes shaken my reasons for the faith which is*
> *in me. But my heart has always assured and reassured me that*
> *the gospel of Jesus Christ must be a divine reality. The Sermon*
> *on the Mount cannot be a mere human production. This belief*
> *enters into the very depth of my conscience. The whole history*
> *of man proves it.*

Webster became convinced that only a genuine Christian could live the Sermon on the Mount. Only through the power of the Holy Spirit can a person live this kind of life.

A New Section in the Sermon:

When we come to Matthew 5:13, we come to a new section of the Sermon on the Mount. We now pass from an abstract definition of the Christian to a functional one. There is a difference between these two, an abstract definition and a functional definition. The second gives an understanding of a term in action. In these further definitions of the Christian, Jesus is saying that while it is true that the Christian is poor in spirit, mournful for sin, gentile, thirsty for righteousness, merciful, pure in heart, a peacemaker and persecuted, nevertheless, he is never to be these things in isolation from a natural and sharply antithetical world. Instead, he is to manifest those characteristics in the world. And what is more, he is to practice these things in a way that will affect the world positively, as salt affects the medium to which one applies it.

In this passage, Jesus talks about the influence Christians are to have on his world. Different Christians influence their world differently and separately. I recently read about a young, mentally disabled boy who was a member of Tabernacle Baptist Church in Atlanta, Georgia. Even though he was a little different and had zeal without knowledge, he was a Christian and greatly desired to see souls come to Christ. Once, at the end of the sermon, when the pastor appealed to people for salvation, this young man drew up alongside a well-dressed young man and asked him, "Do you want to go to heaven?" Bluntly, the young man barked out, "NO!"

"Go to hell, then!" said our young evangelist as he walked away. God's Holy Spirit used that boy's sincere effort to awaken the haughty sinner's slumbering soul. That day, he chose Christ as his Savior and heaven as his eternal home. Jesus is telling us we should have a similar influence. He does that by using two illustrations to convince us.

THE SALT OF THE EARTH

Jesus' use of salt is most interesting because salt is a wonder. Salt is composed of two poisonous substances. How is it possible that salt, which is necessary to live, is composed of sodium and chloride, either of which, if taken individually, would kill you? Yet, the combination makes the product valuable, even necessary to our existence. Further, Jesus uses this to show our eternal influence on the world and its people.

It will help us to focus more clearly on this illustration of salt if we understand its significant uses, especially those most valued in ancient times:

- **Salt is Most Used as a Preservative:**

There were no refrigerators in Jesus' day, no freezer units. Further, the Mediterranean world was primarily tropical. In such a climate, people used salt to keep food from rotting, particularly meat. With the salt, it could resist spoilage and keep putrefaction at bay. So when Jesus said, *You are the salt of the earth,* He meant the world apart from God is rotten because of sin, but through His power, His disciples were able and obligated to have a preserving and purifying effect upon it.

A clear understanding of this principle will keep us from two significant errors accompanying problems expressing the Christian's social responsibilities. The first error is the thought that the world is basically good and will gradually become better and even perfect through Christian social action. Yet even though the world appears healthy for a time, it is dead spiritually.

The second error is the view that because the world is rotten, the Christian should try to disassociate himself from it as much as possible, retreating to a monastery or one of our white (or black), middle-class, self-protecting churches, and let the world go on its way. The answer to this error is that God means for the Christian to be a preserving force in the world wherever He places him.

That means we must allow God to rub us into the world. It means the Christian must be at work, politics, home, and everywhere else moral life in society takes them. We must get out of the saltshaker and spread around. It means we may get dirty, perhaps dissolve, and even disappear. The fact is that salt must dissolve to preserve anything.

- **It Provides Flavor:**

Food without salt is sadly bland and often even sickening. You know what value salt is to food if you can't have any. The Christian, through the life of Jesus, is to lend flavor to a flavorless, tasteless world. Christianity is to life what salt is to food. The tragedy is that often people have associated Christianity with precisely the opposite. They have connected Christianity with that which takes the flavor out of life. So, Christians walk around with long faces, unable to have any fun" in life. The world becomes gray because of Christianity.

The nineteenth-century poet and critic A.C. Swinburne said, "Thou hast conquered, O pale Galilean; the world has grown grey from thy breath."

Oliver Wendell Holmes once said, "I might have entered the ministry if certain clergymen I knew had not looked and acted so much like undertakers."

In his diary, Robert Louis Stevenson wrote, as if a remarkable fact, "I have been to church today, and am not depressed."

Those are honest remarks by people who have seen an insipid Christianity. And if they and their followers are to see something different, they must see it in the only place it can or will be seen––in us. Do we go around with long faces as if the world and everything we know are depressing? Or do we go about as those who bear within the Spirit of the Living God? The second is our true responsibility, whereby we show forth the flavor of Christ and Christianity.

- **Salt Makes One Thirsty:**

The third thing salt does is make a person thirsty. This purpose leads us to ask ourselves, "Do I make people thirsty for Jesus Christ?" The non-Christian tends to feel self-satisfied even if he is not. So he naturally goes through life telling himself that circumstances are lovely. But when a Christian comes into his vision, there should be that evidence of joy, satisfaction, and peace that makes him look up and say, "That's what I want; that is what I want to be like!" Can that be said of you? Do you make men thirsty for Jesus Christ?

In ancient times during the Feast of Tabernacles in the city of Jerusalem, it was the custom for the priest to go to the Siloam pool each day and return bearing large containers of water to empty upon the altar in the Temple. They did this for seven days during the feast and repeated the ceremony seven times on the last day. On that day, during the Feast of Tabernacles in the year that He attended, Jesus Christ stood and cried in a loud voice, *If any man is thirsty, let him come to Me and drink. He who believes in Me, as the Scripture said, 'From his innermost being shall flow rivers of living water,'* (John 7:37-38). Jesus Christ can indeed satisfy the thirst of the human soul.

Our responsibility is not to quench our thirst with things of this world but to point men to Jesus Christ.

- **Salt is a Common Substance:**

Salt is one of the most common things in life. When Jesus said, *"You are the salt of the earth,"* He meant, "I delight to use little things." He did not say, "You are the gold or uranium of the earth." He said "salt," a common substance. He chooses to use common things from the weak, foolish, despised, and things not rare or significant, to bring the greatest glory to His name (I Corinthians 1:26-29).

When God called Moses to lead His people out of Egypt, He did not speak in a dazzling theophany, use thunder, lightning, or a powerful vision. Instead, He revealed Himself in a burning desert bush.

When David was to deliver Israel from Philistine tyranny, God did not use guns and bombs, not even Saul's armor. Instead, He used a sling and a few small stones.

When Jesus was born, God did not allow His birth in the courts of the Caesars or of a woman of noble ancestry and great culture. Instead, He chose a peasant girl, who was probably illiterate, and she gave birth to Jesus Christ in a stable.

God uses small things and small people. He uses you and me so that He might do His work in the world. The smaller we can become, the more effective His work in us will be.

- **Useless Salt:**

Jesus says, *but if the salt has become tasteless, how will it be made salty again? It is good for nothing anymore, except to be thrown out and trampled underfoot by men.* In Palestine, the people build ordinary outdoor stone ovens on a tile base. A thick salt bed is laid under the tile floor in such ovens to retain the heat. After a certain length of time, the salt perishes. They take up the tiles, remove the salt and throw it on the road. They throw out the salt when it loses its power to heat the tiles. That may well be the picture here. But the essential point remains whatever the view, and it is a point the New Testament makes repeatedly––uselessness invites disaster! If a Christian is not fulfilling his purpose as a Christian, then he is on the way to disaster. God means for us to be the salt of the earth, and if we do not bring to life the purity, the antiseptic power, the radiance that we ought, then we invite disaster.

THE LIGHT OF THE WORLD

The second illustration Jesus uses of the functional definition of Christianity and the Christian's influence on the world is light. We need to look at these words carefully because they are profound. There are essential implications involved.

The Darkened World:

The first clear implication of Christ's words is that the world is in the dark where spiritual things are concerned. The tragedy of the situation is that men prefer darkness to God's light. Jesus was the world's light and now Christians are the world's light. Therefore, His words compliment the Christian because the Christian is what Jesus is.

Many years ago, *Time Magazine* made some accurate remarks about the presence of sin and evil in America:

> *It is the particular heresy of Americans that they see themselves as potential saints more than as real-life sinners. Today's young radicals, in particular, are almost painfully sensitive to these*

*and other wrongs of their society and denounce them violently.
But at the same time, they are typically American in that they
fail to place evil in its historic and human perspective. To them,
evil is not an irreducible component of man, an inescapable
fact of life, but something committed by the older generation,
attributable to a particular class of the establishment, and
eradicable through love and revolution.*

This article appeared in December of 1969 and is as true today as it was then. Something deceived Americans, as well as all mankind into thinking they are not real sinners. Very few people place sin and evil in the proper perspective because they are all part of a darkened world. The world is blind to the reality of sin and evil.

We are the Light of the World:

What do we do with a world of darkness like that? We put the light in it! In John 9:5, Jesus said, *As long as I am in the world, I am the light of the world.* When He commanded His followers to be the lights of the world, He demanded nothing less than that they should be like Himself. In himself, the Christian cannot be the light of the world. However, he can show forth light to the extent that he first receives it from the Lord Jesus Christ and reflects it from Him to others. This passage describes the Christian as a lamp or a candle. He gives forth light. But he does so only because he first has been kindled by Jesus. In John's gospel, John the Baptist is described as *a burning and a shining lamp* by Jesus. The point is that John's light is secondary to Christ; John's is a kindled light and exists only because of Christ.

Dr. Donald Grey Barnhouse often used the best and most excellent illustration on this point I have heard. He used to say that when Christ was in the world, He was a bit like the sun, which is here by day and gone by night. But when the sun goes down, the moon comes up, and the moon is a picture of the Church, of Christians. It shines, but it does not shine by its own light.

It only shines because it reflects the light of the sun. Jesus said that He was the world's light, but He knew He would leave the world, so He said, *You are the light of the world!*

A City Cannot be Hidden:

People understand the need to see the light, so Jesus talks about a city on a hill. People could always see a city in the dark if it sat on a hill in Palestine. There can be no such thing as secret discipleship, for either the secrecy destroys the discipleship, or the discipleship destroys the secrecy. A man's Christianity should be obvious to all men. Further, this Christianity should not be visible only within the Church. Christianity whose effects stop at the Church door is useless to everyone. It should be even more visible in our ordinary activities, in how we treat our fellow workers, order in a restaurant, treat our employees, serve our employer, play a game, drive a car, everyday language, and in the things we read. A Christian must be as much a Christian on the job, in the classroom, the kitchen, the golf course, or the playing field as in the Church.

Shining for God:

We are the world's light, and Jesus illustrates that in two ways, the city on the hill and the lamp placed under a peck measure. Verse 16 shows us just how we allow that light to shine. What should be the result of this influence on the world?

- **Men Must See Our Good Deeds.** The Greek word Jesus uses for "good" is Kalos, which also means winsome, beautiful, and attractive. So, the good deeds of the Christian must be good indeed, but they must also be attractive. In other words, Christianity has a specific and unique kind of goodness. The tragedy of much so-called goodness is the element of hardness, coldness, and austerity. There is a goodness that attracts and

87

a goodness that repels. There is a charm in Christian goodness which makes it a lovely thing.

- **Our Light Should Glorify God.** Our light and deeds should not draw attention to ourselves but to God. The goodness which draws attention to itself is not Christian.

- The Christian never thinks of what he has done but only what God has enabled him to do. Therefore, he never seeks to draw the eyes of men to himself but always directs them to God.

What Does the World see?

Do men see Jesus Christ in you? They will not find him in the world because the world is dark. They will not find him in the world's literature, culture, or pastimes. They will see Him only as you look to Jesus, as you spend time with Him, allowing some of His light to reflect from your life to those about you

Review and Resolve:

1. How do this lesson and these verses begin a new section in the Sermon on the Mount?
2. What are the two primary errors in expressing the Christian's social responsibilities?
3. How can your life or our church provide flavor for the people in our community?
4. What can we do to make the people in our community thirsty for Jesus Christ?
5. What did you think of the illustration from Dr. Donald Grey Barnhouse?
6. What should be the result of the influence of our light in the world?
7. Name one thing you can do this week to become salt.

Chapter 11

Christ and the Law

Do not think that I came to abolish the Law or the Prophets. I did not come to abolish, but to fulfill. For truly I say to you, until heaven and earth pass away, not the smallest letter or stroke shall pass away from the Law, until all is accomplished. Whoever then annuls one of the least of these commandments, and so teaches others, shall be called least in the kingdom of heaven; but whoever keeps and teaches them, he shall be called great in the kingdom of heaven. For I say to you, that unless your righteousness surpasses that of the scribes and Pharisees, you shall not enter the kingdom of heaven (Matthew 5:17-20)

The noted 18th-century French philosopher Voltaire said it took centuries to build up Christianity, but "I'll show how just one Frenchman can destroy it within fifty years." Then, taking his pen, he dipped it into the ink of unbelief and wrote against God.

Twenty years after his death, the Geneva Bible Society purchased his house for printing the Bible. And it later became the Paris headquarters for the British and Foreign Bible Society. The Bible is still a best-seller. It is interesting, in contrast, that someone once sold an entire six-volume set of Voltaire's works for ninety cents. Just before his death, the noted atheist swore: "I wish I had never been born!"

Others have attempted to destroy the Bible. Thomas Paine, an immigrant to America in 1787, wrote his masterpiece, *The Age of Reason* which scoffed Christianity and the Bible. He said his work "would destroy the Bible. Within 100 years, Bibles will be found only in museums or in musty corners of second-hand bookstores." His book was published in London in 1794 and brought him so much misery and loneliness that he said: "I would give worlds, if I had them, had the *Age of Reason* never been written." He became bedridden until his death in 1809, friendless and alone. However, the Bible remained a best-seller.

Jesus talked about the Scriptures, and I am sure those who were listening were interested in what He had to say. Jesus is talking here about the Old Testament, the Law. First, the Law constantly confronted these people. In that day the Jewish Law contained some 613 commandments. Today there are those in the church who would have difficulty naming even the Ten Commandments. Think how it would be if we had 613 laws with which to deal! Second, Jesus had already become known as a lawbreaker, and we may be sure these people wanted to see how He would defend Himself.

This text is essential because of what it has to say about righteousness. However, it also highlights the relationship between the New Testament and the Old Testament, between the Gospel and the Law. It divides itself nicely into Christ and the Law (vs. 17-18) and the Christian and the Law (vs. 19-20).

This passage is fascinating. It seems that Jesus broke the Law of the Jews again and again. For example, He did not observe the hand washings that the Law laid down; He healed sick people on the Sabbath, although the Law forbade such healings. He was condemned and crucified as a lawbreaker, yet here seems to speak of the Law with veneration and reverence that no Rabbi or Pharisee could exceed. Let's observe what He says here. For our discussion, we will give attention to four points.

The Purpose of Christ's Coming (Verse 17).

Notice the first thing Jesus says is He came with a mission. He did not come to abolish the Law and the prophets, set them aside, or even endorse them in a dead and literalistic way. Instead, He came to fulfill them.

The verb translated "to fulfill" literally means "to fill" and indicates that Christ's sayings were no appeal of the former but a drawing out and filling up of them. To grasp the far-reaching implications of this, we need to recall that "the Law and the prophets," namely the Old Testament, contain various kinds of teaching. We can see that Jesus had a relationship of fulfillment with them all.

Doctrinal Teaching. The Old Testament contains doctrinal teaching, which is called the "Torah," usually translated as "Law," meaning "revealed instruction." All the great Biblical doctrines are there. Yet it was only a partial revelation. Jesus fulfilled it all through His person, teaching, and work. Bishop Ryle said: "The Old Testament is the Gospel in the bud, the New Testament is the Gospel in full flower. The Old Testament is the Gospel in the blade; the New Testament is the Gospel in full ear."

Predictive Prophecy. The Old Testament contains predictive prophecy, which looks forward to the days of the Messiah. It either foretells Him in word or foreshadows Him in type. Yet, this was only anticipation. Jesus fulfilled it all, so what the Scriptures predicted came to pass in Him. The first statement of His public ministry declares this: *The time is fulfilled, and the kingdom of God is at hand* (Mark 1:15). His very words say, *I have come!* Again and again, He claimed that the Scriptures bore witness of Him. Matthew emphasizes this more than any of the other Gospel writers by his repeated formula, *All this took place to fulfill what the Lord had spoken by the prophets ...* The climax was His death on the cross in which the whole ceremonial system of the Old Testament, both priesthood and sacrifice, found its perfect fulfillment. Then the ceremonies ceased. This fulfillment abolished their use because Christ fully confirmed their meaning. They were but a "Shadow" of what was to come; the "substance" belonged to Christ.

Ethical Precepts. The Old Testament contained the ethical precepts or the moral Law of God. They were often misunderstood and disobeyed. Jesus fulfilled them in the first instance by obeying every one of them, for He was ... *born under the law,* and was determined ... *to fulfill all righteousness* (Galatians 4:4; Matthew 3:15).

The purpose of Jesus was not to change the law, still less to annul it, but to reveal the full depth of its intended meaning. He does that by fulfilling the Law Himself. The attitude of the Lord Jesus about the Old Testament was not one of destruction and discontinuity but instead of a constructive, organic continuity. He summed up His position in a single word, not "abolition" but "fulfillment."

The Perseverance of the Law (Verse 18).

The statement which Jesus makes in verse 18 confirms for us once again that the Bible is inspired right down to the very smallest particle. The words "smallest letter" is called a "jot" by the KJV and refers to the Hebrew letter "iodh." (Surely, you have heard of iodh, a very small person from the Star Wars movies!) In form, it is like an apostrophe and refers to the smallest possible particle in Hebrew. It is not even a letter or much bigger than a dot. Not even a dot would pass away.

The word "stroke," called a "tittle" in the KJV, is what we call the "serif." This serif is the tiny projecting part at the foot of a letter, the little line at each side of the foot, for example, the letter "I." Jesus says the law is so sacred that no minor detail will ever disappear.

We need to remember we are dealing with God's Word. Men wrote the Bible under the inspiration of God. What they wrote says what God says. Thus, we equate the Scriptures with God's Words (Acts 3:25; Romans 9:15). It is the sole authority for the Christian and the Church. It is the only standard of authority for faith (what we believe) and practice (what we are to do). It is God's Word to man. *Thus saith the Lord* is found 1900 times in the Old Testament, written mostly by the Prophets. Phrases like *The Lord said, The Lord spoke, and The Word of the Lord came* appear 3,808 times in the Old Testament. That means 5,708 clear statements declare this to be God's Word.

The New Testament contains 280 quotations from 30 of the 39 Old Testament books. Moreover, we find these quotations across 18 of the 27 New Testament books. In other words, the Old and New Testaments have a very close relationship.

None of the Word of God will pass away. He says not a single letter, or part of a letter, will pass away until heaven and the earth themselves pass away. Then, they will pass away one day, and the Scriptures will still stand. The Law of God is more enduring than the universe. It is the only eternal thing you and I can handle with our hands in this life. Do we believe that? We should because Jesus taught it. As Christians, we cannot remain faithful to His teaching and say, "I like the Sermon on the Mount, but I don't like the references to the blood of Jesus Christ; they offend me." We cannot say, "I like prophecy, but then neglect Christ's ethics." We cannot say, "I like the New Testament, but not the Old Testament." "I like certain things Jesus said, but not others Christ said." We must take it all. Paul taught that *All Scripture is given by inspiration of God, and is profitable for doctrine, for reproof, for correction, for instruction in righteousness* (II Timothy 3:16).

The Prediction for Those Using the Law (Verse 19).

The word "Therefore" (KJV) introduces the deduction that Jesus now draws for His disciples from the enduring validity of the Law and His attitude concerning it. It reveals a vital connection between the law of God and the kingdom of God. Because He has come, not to abolish, but to fulfill the

Law, and because not an "iota" or "dot" will pass from the Law until all has been fulfilled, "therefore" greatness in the kingdom of God will be measured by conformity to it. Notice also that personal obedience is not enough. Christian disciples must also teach others the permanently binding nature of the Law's commandments.

True, not all the commandments are equally "weighty." Yet even one of the least of these commandments, precisely because it is a commandment of God the King, is important. To relax it and loosen its hold on our conscience and authority, is an offense to God, whose law it is. To disregard a "least" commandment in the Law (in either obedience or instruction) is to demote oneself to the "least" subject in the kingdom. In other words, greatness in the kingdom of God belongs to those who are faithful in doing and teaching the whole moral law of God.

The Bible clarifies that there is a judgment upon those who would take away or add to God's Word. Revelation 22:18-19 speaks to this: *If anyone adds to them, God shall add to him the plagues which are written in this book; and if anyone takes away from the words of the book of this prophecy, God shall take away his part from the tree of life and from the holy city which are written in this book.*

The Prescription For Righteousness (Verse 20).

We have already spoken of this verse to some extent. It is a crucial verse because it gives the heart of the Sermon on the Mount. Jesus goes further here than in the previous verse. Not only is greatness in the kingdom assessed by a righteousness that conforms to the Law, but entry into the kingdom is impossible without conformity better (much better: the Greek expression is very emphatic) than that of the Scribes and Pharisees. But, indeed, someone would protest. The Scribes and Pharisees were famous for their righteousness. Was not obedience to God's law the master passion of their lives? Did they not calculate that the Law contains 248 commandments and 365 prohibitions, and did they not aspire to keep them all?

How can Christian righteousness exceed pharisaic righteousness, and how can this superior Christian righteousness be made a condition of entering God's kingdom? Does this not teach a doctrine of salvation by good works and contradict the first beatitude, which says the kingdom belongs to *the poor in spirit* who have nothing, not even righteousness, to plead?

One need not seek far for the answer to all these questions. Christian righteousness far surpasses pharisaic righteousness in kind rather than in degree. It is not so much that Christians keep some 613 laws but that Christian righteousness is deeper, being the righteousness of the heart. The Pharisees were content with external and formal obedience and rigid conformity to the letter of the Law. Jesus teaches us that God's demands are far more radical than this. The righteousness pleasing to Him is an inward righteousness of the mind and a person's motives. For *The Lord looks on the heart* (I Samuel 16:7; Luke 16:15).

C.S. Lewis once said, "How little people know who think that righteousness is dull. When one meets the real thing, it is irresistible."

Review and Resolve:

1. What is the most important thing about this paragraph of Scripture?
2. What is the primary purpose of Christ's coming to earth?
3. How did Jesus fulfill the:
    A. Doctrinal Teaching (Torah)
    B. Predictive Prophecies
    C. Ethical Precepts
4. Explain in your own words what Jesus teaches about Scripture in verse 18.
5. Describe what Jesus would consider a righteous man.
6. What is most important about righteousness?

Chapter 12

Three Quiet Ways to Commit Murder

You have heard that the ancients were told, 'You shall not commit murder' and 'Whoever commits murder shall be liable to the court.' But I say to you that everyone who is angry with his brother shall be guilty before the court; and whoever shall say to his brother, 'Raca,' shall be guilty before the supreme court; and whoever shall say, 'You fool,' shall be guilty enough to go into the hell of fire (Matthew 21:22).

Have you ever noticed our tendency to come as close as possible to the border of sin? We will go as far as we can go without actually sinning sometimes. And then, other times, we cannot stop at the boundary line. As a result, we attempt to justify ourselves by modifying or playing dumb to the commandments of Scripture.

We believe some of the statements we make to ourselves and others in this time of compromise, explain away our actions. Here are a few of the classics. Maybe you will recognize some of them:

- "What's wrong with immorality as long as we aren't hurting anyone else? As long as it is between two consenting adults, how can it be wrong?"

- "I know it's' a weakness, but ..."
- "I have tried, but I just can't seem to help myself, so I give up."
- "Well, it sure doesn't bother me, and I just don't care what other people think."
- "That's just the kind of person I am. I call them like I see them. You may not like what I say, but at least you'll always know where I stand on every issue."
- "This is really a busy time of the year for me, so don't expect me to be very faithful."
- "I know God's Word says I shouldn't worry or fret, but I am just so concerned about how this will work out."
- "You just have to get used to me. I'll never change, so like it or lump it. What you see is what you get."
- "Surely God doesn't expect me to be faithful in my attendance in church or my giving to the church when I have so many bills. As soon as I get out of debt, I'll begin to give again."
- "I defend my homosexual lifestyle because I was born that way."

These statements are not new. In one form or another, they have been with us from the beginning of man. Some are honest reflections, and some even have a measure of truth. For the most part, however, they are attempts to justify or explain away sinful behavior. They are a clever sidestepping of obedience.

When we do this, it could be devastating to our spiritual health. We must avoid explaining why we are not compliant with the Word of God. That is precisely what the Pharisees did. They dedicated themselves to the Law but added rules and regulations. They also went to the opposite extreme and gave excuses for not going as far as the spirit of the Law intended. They wanted to find the Law more suitable to their interpretation.

The famous British preacher, John R.W. Stott, captures the Pharisees' attitude well: "The Pharisees were trying to reduce the challenge of the Law, to relax (Matthew 5:10) the commands of God and make His moral demands more manageable and less exacting. They were attempting to make the Law's demands less demanding and the Law's permission more permissive."

Stott goes on: "Jesus reversed both tendencies. He insisted instead, that the full implication of God's commands must be accepted without imposing artificial limits, whereas the limits which God had set to His permission must be accepted and not arbitrarily increased."

All of this leads us to a fundamental principle. The Pharisees were very concerned about outward obedience to the Law. However, we must understand "Ethics involves not only an external act but also a heart attitude." Out heart intention is the primary focus for ethical decisions. Therefore, ethics involves more than conformity to rules. This heart intention is what the Pharisees missed.

Beginning with this passage, Jesus follows up on verse 20 where He says our righteousness must surpass that of the Pharisees, which means it must be the righteousness of the heart. He teaches in this section that the original purpose of the Law intended to include the heart. For instance, the Pharisees:

1. Limited adultery to an act. Therefore, Jesus will show it in the heart.
2. Limited the commands about swearing and honesty to certain oaths involving God's name. Jesus will call for truthfulness and exactness in every area of speech.
3. Only limited the commands about loving neighbors to certain people. Jesus will broaden it to include unlovable people and even our enemies.
4. Limited murder to the actual premeditated act. Jesus will show "three quiet ways to commit murder."

What Jesus is going to do is to reveal the heart of God rather than the letter of the Law. He introduces much of this discussion with the familiar phrase, *You have heard that it was said ... but I say unto you....* He will use this formula six times in this chapter. In each case, He refers to the Law or a Pharisaic addition to the Law, and then He reveals the heart of God in the matter. He thus shows us how our righteousness must exceed the righteousness of the Scribes and Pharisees. Using this formula, Jesus takes all sin to our hearts, attitudes, and motives. He takes it all deeper than the letter of the Law.

Further, the formula is very emphatic. The Greek words "ego de lego" literally mean, *I, even I, say to you.* Jesus is not overriding the law here, nor is He superseding it. However, He is placing a new and deeper emphasis on it and showing that a man can still sin even though he keeps the letter of the Law. This depth makes this Sermon on the Mount a bit devastating, even crushing to the listener.

The Primary Cause of Murder:

The first and unmistakable kind of murder is the deliberate ending of one's life (5:21). This is still a valid commandment. It was first given in Genesis 9:6, *Whoever sheds the blood of man, by man shall his blood be shed; for in the image of God has God made man.* The command is also given to us in Exodus 20:13 and Deuteronomy 5:17. Even though the KJV uses the word "Kill," the original language is closer to the idea of "murder." It is premeditated murder with malice and revenge as the motive. It is the unlawful killing of another human being––homicide.

We should note that not all killing is murder. If you hit and kill a boy on a bicycle because he suddenly comes out from a side street, that is not murder. It is an accident. There was no malice, no premeditation on your part. Of course, you feel despair and anguish over the tragedy, but you will not be a murderer.

Why is premeditated and revengeful murder so serious? Here is the key! *Man is created in God's own image* (Genesis 9:6). Notice the implications:

1. If we murder, we "take on God" personally, and He will hold us accountable because we have taken His place.
2. If we seek to take another person's life, we see them as without worth, as worthless. Can that be if Genesis 9:6 is true?
3. We don't see our worth if we seek to kill someone. As a result, we do not appreciate the actual value of our own life.
4. If we are tragically misled and seek to take the life of an unborn child, we violate the spirit of the Law that sees all human life, born and unborn, as made in the image of God. It is taking the place of God, devaluating His image, and breaking the commandment. It is a modern-day example of Phariseeism. It seeks to make the laws of God manageable and palatable while avoiding the spirit of the Law.

If we fail and repent, there is no condemnation for those in Christ Jesus. God dealt with our sins through His forgiveness. But, the nation that makes laws to purposely and with forethought end life will come under the judgment of God. This nation will be held accountable for what they have done. Our nation, Christians, and non-Christians alike, will feel the rain of God's wrath for this present violation of His law. Please make no mistake about it. If God doesn't, He will have to apologize to Sodom and Gomorrah.

The Quiet Variety, ANGER:

If Jesus had asked the Pharisees how many of them had committed murder, not one of them would have said he did. They might have killed a few mosquitoes, but never a person. However, the Lord challenges that stance by taking them beyond the letter to the spirit of the law. He shows them that the physical act of murder results from something that starts in the heart.

The Pharisees thought they were doing well up to this point. Perhaps we, too, are shocked at these statements. However, he shows an unusual authority with *"But I say to you ..."* (Verse 22). He does not contradict Moses but shows what Moses had in mind when he gave the Law.

There are two words that Jesus might have used for anger. One is the word "thumos." This word is anger that quickly blazes up, and just as quickly, dies down. It represents a more agitated condition of feelings. It is an outburst of wrath. It is the kind of anger most of us have experienced. First, we boil up in a rage, and then it is over. It is like getting a flat and kicking the tire in frustration and tension. Then it's "Oh, nuts," or "Oh, $%#&@*^," and you're through it.

The second word is the word "orgizo." Jesus uses this word here, and the definition differs from that of thumos.

1. It is more long-lived anger.
2. It's the anger of a man who nurses it to keep it warm.
3. It's anger for which a person broods. It's a strong feeling of displeasure that he will keep alive (Words like rage, fury, and indignation are synonyms for this anger).
4. It is a more settled and abiding condition of the mind and frequently seeks revenge because it has turned into pure bitterness
5. It wants to get at the person who has wronged them, and harm the person psychologically, mentally, or even physically. There is an impulse to retaliate! Jesus is saying that the person who has this kind of anger has committed a kind of murder. We are accountable for these outbursts as a murderer because, in God's sight, that is murder. 1 John 3:15 says: *Anyone who hates his brother is a murderer, and you know that no murderer has eternal life in him.*

The outcome of this kind of anger is people get hurt. Three people can get hurt. First is the person with whom we are angry. We can inflict physical or emotional scars inflicted on them. Don't forget words can kill. Second, innocent people may get caught in the wake or the aftershock of our anger. And third, and most often, we get hurt. This anger boils in our emotions and, if unchecked, will destroy us. It not only destroys our relationship with others, but it is also suicide. It becomes a death wish for us. And we must not forget the judgment of God upon us as a result.

The Second Quiet Verity, INSULTS:

The second quiet way to commit murder is by using insults. "Raca" is a difficult word to translate because it involves an insult (derogatory term) and describes a tone of voice. We use it with a degrading, hostile, unloving, tone. More specifically, "raca" can mean the following four things:

1. It is a term that demeans another person's mental capabilities. Like calling a person a "meathead, numbskull, blockhead, airhead, dummy, stupid, or He's got toys in the attic.
2. We can use it for blocks of people and ethnic slurs. "Jew boy, dumb Arab, whitey, drunken Indian, Pollock." These insults are demeaning to a person's character.
3. It can also be directed toward another person as a "swear word" (I won't attempt to illustrate).
4. We can use it as "sick humor." It's running a person down through a joke of humor. For example, "He's two sandwiches short of a picnic."

These kinds of insults tend to freeze a person out of an association. Somehow, they are not worth our time. It is a form of murder because it denies a person the possibility of fulfillment. It completely disregards the fact that God made this person in His image. It also puts scars on his mind and heart for life. It also causes others to form opinions, not from their observation but yours.

This kind of insult, Jesus says, deserves the judgment of spiritual leaders if it persists and goes unchecked. The procedure today is not the Sanhedrin but the church. Galatians 6:1 and Matthew 18:15-17 are the processes for today for both parties, the one offending and the one who is offended.

The Third Quiet Verity--CALL A PERSON A FOOL:

This type is one of the worst kinds of quiet murder. It is more than calling someone a bad name or letting off steam. The word used for "fool" is the word "moros," from which we get our English word "moron." The word had a different connotation then than it does today. It was, in effect, calling a person a moral fool. Therefore, it is a judgment of a person's inner character or heart. It says this person has no capacity for proper thought or action. Therefore, denies him all confidence and fellowship. It could mean an apostate or an outcast.

There is a difference between RACA and MOROS. Raca expresses contempt for a man's head, "you are stupid." Moros expresses contempt for his heart and character, "You are a scoundrel."

The judgment for this kind of murder is *"fiery hell."* The New Testament uses different words for hell, but the most popular term is "Gehenna." We know from Biblical history this is the valley of Hinnom (S.W. of Jerusalem). This valley is where King Ahaz introduced the burning of children to the pagan god Moleck (II Kings 23:10; II Chronicles 28:3; 33:6; Jeremiah 7:31; 32:35). King Josiah later stopped the practice and ordered the valley be accursed. Therefore, it became Jerusalem's city dump. There was always a smoldering fire at Gehenna to dispose of the trash. To this place of fire and garbage, Jesus says a person who drags down another person's name will go. It is the fires of hell.

He is telling the disciples and us that the gravest thing is to destroy a man's reputation, which is behind calling a person a name. Therefore, any attempt to kill a man's name is an attempt to murder him, which calls for the most severe judgment possible.

Conclusion:

Angry thoughts, insulting words, and defaming of character may never lead to the ultimate physical act of murder. Yet they are equivalent to murder in God's sight. Satan's attempts to destroy and kill do not always come from the outside. Often his plans include the murder coming from our brothers and sisters in Christ. So don't give him the victory, and don't rob yourself of a right standing with God.

Each of us should, right now, ask God and ourselves if we are guilty of murder. If we are, then we need to settle it quickly. If we are not, but we are the object of someone's anger, we need to fix that for our name's sake and the spiritual health of the other person.

Right now, each of us should also go from this place, not in condemnation, but as being sent by God to bring peace. God wants us to be free from every emotional and relational debt. Go in God's strength to do His work of peace.

Review and Resolve:

1. What is the primary ethical issue, as stated in this lesson?
2. What was the problem with the thinking of the Pharisees when it came to the Law?
3. Give two of the implications that make murder so severe.
4. Why is the anger that Jesus talks about so serious, and what are some of the implications of such anger?
5. Can you give a few illustrations of modern-day insults?
6. Why do you think such severe judgment comes upon someone who calls a man a fool?
7. What can you resolve to do this week to comply with Jesus' instruction?

Chapter 13

The Prevention of Murder

If therefore you are presenting your offering at the altar, and there remember that your brother has something against you, leave your offering there before the altar, and go your way; first, be reconciled to your brother, and then come and present your offering. Make friends quickly with your opponent at law while you are with him on the way, in order that your opponent may not deliver you to the judge, and the judge to the officer, and you be thrown into prison. Truly I say to you, you shall not come out of there until you have paid up the last cent (Matthew 5:23-26).

Will Rogers once said: "People who fly into a rage always make a bad landing!" This quote is good for all of us! We cannot save face if we lose our heads!

The great Maestro, Toscanini, was as well-known for his ferocious temper as for his outstanding musicianship. When his orchestra members played poorly, he picked up anything in sight and hurled it to the floor. During one rehearsal, a flat note caused the genius to grab his valuable watch and smash it beyond repair. Shortly afterward, he received from his devoted musicians a luxurious velvet-lined box containing two watches, one a beautiful gold timepiece, the other a cheap one on which was inscribed, "For Rehearsals Only."

The Lord now tells us what to do with our anger. He begins in Matthew 5:23 to show how to prevent the murder discussed in 5:21-22. The words *"If therefore,"* bring us back to the previous passage with a practical application of that teaching. In His application of verses 21-22, Jesus shows two ways a person may be reconciled to another person to prevent murder. Though these two illustrations come from His culture, we understand them today.

Jesus' theme in these verses is, "If anger, insult, and character assassination are so serious and dangerous, we must avoid them like the plaque and speedily take action." He first illustrates our relationship with God (verses 23-24). The second illustration concerns our relationship with other people (verses 25-26). As we have said, Jesus expressed them in the cultural terms of His day where the temple still stood, and they offered sacrifices. Therefore, we will translate His illustrations into a slightly more modern dress.

Relationship With God (5:23-24).

As we read the Bible, we know the chief tragedy of sin is that it separates men from God. It breaks the relationship. The whole purpose of the sacrifice upon the altar was to restore that broken relationship, Still, suppose one had a fractured relationship with his brother. In that case, he could not hope to restore a relationship with God until he first restored his relationship with his brother.

You say, "Oh, but wasn't the meaning of the sacrifice in that it atoned for sin and covered the guilt of the one presenting it?" The answer is yes! However, God never meant sacrifice to excuse the necessity for restitution! To ask God to forgive us and not provide the necessary restitution is meaningless repentance. We see this in Scripture.

We must never forget King David was a saved man in heaven today because he looked for the Messiah he knew was coming to save men from sin. Still, when he wrote of his daily relationship with God and his sin, he said, *If I regard iniquity in my heart, the LORD will not hear me* (Psalm 66:18).

Samuel said to King Saul on the occasion of Saul's first great disobedience to the Lord after he was king, *Hath the LORD great delight in burnt offerings and sacrifices, as in obeying the voice of the LORD? Behold, to obey is better than sacrifice, and to hearken than the fat of rams* (I Samuel 15:22).

Offering at the Altar:

Jesus, of course, is putting all this in that culture. We need to apply it to ourselves. We no longer go to the temple and offer sacrifices on the altar as the Jews did then. We must update these words in our worship process. We might say, "When you come into a church gathering, or before God in worship or prayer." If you are in the middle of a church service and remember your brother has a grievance against you, leave the church immediately and put it right. Do not wait until the service ends. Seek out your brother and ask his forgiveness. First, go and be reconciled to your brother, then come and offer your worship to God.

Taking the Initiative:

We should notice here that the righting of offences is always to be our initiative, regardless of who is right or wrong. So, in the text, you will see it says if we remember someone else has something against us, even though we don't have the same negative feelings, we are still obligated to bring about reconciliation, if possible.

We will see this means we are our brother's keeper. If someone else is out of fellowship with us, we are to seek reconciliation and then come and worship. It puts the obligation of reconciliation and peace on us regardless of the circumstances. So, if you are praying in church, don't wait until you finish.

Seek out your brother and ask him first for reconciliation. Then return to your place or the prayer meeting.

A Statement of Priority:

It seems God is laying down a priority for us to go by in our relationship with Him. Jesus may be saying one cannot be right with God until he is right with his fellow man. That seems to be the case. Therefore, worshipping God is meaningless as long as an unrepaired human relationship exists in our hearts.

We all know of times when the other person will not accept reconciliation even after one has confessed, apologized, and done everything possible. But that is not the point. We must rid our hearts of the wrong feeling and do all we can to restore the relationship. If the other person refuses a right relationship, at least the one who attempted the restoration is cleared and free to return and kneel before God.

Relationship with People (5:25-26).

The second response shows we are to involve ourselves in peace-making when we are wrong in a relationship. The pictures here are opposites. One is a church scene where brothers need reconciliation, and the other picture is a court scene where enemies need reconciliation. In one picture, we don't feel guilt, but in the other, we are guilty. Verse 26 is a reference to the ancient way of paying a debt. If someone didn't pay their debts, they were put in debtor's prison. That made it tricky to get out of debt.

Settle the Difference Immediately:

One of the major ways to avoid murder in one's heart is to do what we must do immediately, as quickly as possible. Jesus is saying here that sin has consequences, and if you want to avoid the effects, you must confess and correct the wrong as soon as possible. In this sense, the Lord Jesus Christ was only saying in different words what Paul later spoke to the Ephesians: *Be angry, and sin not; let not the sun go down upon your wrath"* (Ephesians 4:26). He also recognized the great principle stated in the 12ᵗʰ chapter of Hebrews: *Follow peace with all men, and holiness ... lest any root of bitterness spring up trouble you, and by it may be defiled* (Hebrews 12:14, 15).

We are to deal with these things immediately. Before someone else comes into the picture and inflicts severe pain upon us, in other words, settle the matter before the judge throws the book at you. We should not wait until we are taken to court or for the judgment of others. Instead, we should try to be reconciled with the person who is right and bringing an accusation against us.

The problem with most of us is if we have a problem with someone else or know someone is mad at us, we put off making peace. We say, "The time is not right," or "I'm not sure that person could handle it now." "Someday, I'll bring that up when it's more convenient." "I can't stand the hassle of it all." Jesus, however, is saying, "Settle matters quickly." It's to the other party's advantage and your advantage if you are guilty.

The Results of Immediate Reconciliation:

We must recognize that immediacy in these matters will help both parties. There are three obvious reasons:

1. It will eliminate mental strain on one or both parties. You will not need to go into a situation or a social meeting with the person and feel the strain and stress between you. You will be free to speak and to love the person because you will know there is nothing wrong between you.

2. If we do not take care of these things, we will stand before God and give account. God knows the more we put it off, the easier it is to justify it. The more distance we get between injustice and reconciliation, the more

chance there is for judgment. Also, if we put it off, it is easier to develop sound arguments to keep us from dealing with the issues. If we settle it quickly, we can eliminate our excuse-making and God's judgment. If we settle it quickly, the loss will only be temporary. We should consider this principle in our immediate and extended family, job, neighborhood, friends, and church.

3. If we immediately settle the matters between us and our friends or enemies, we can eliminate anger, insults, character assassination, and maybe even physical murder from happening. Therefore, this is the cure for murder.

Conclusion:

Someone has said, "Speak well of your enemies; remember, you made them!" We have received forgiveness from God and must willingly give it to other people, no matter what they have done. Allow me to share a true story with you.

During the Korean War, a South Korean Christian, a civilian, was arrested by the communists and ordered shot. But when the young communist leader learned that the prisoner was in charge of an orphanage caring for small children, he decided to spare him and kill his son instead. So, they shot the 19-year-old boy in the presence of his father.

Later the fortunes of war changed, and the United Nations forces captured the young communist leader, tried, and condemned him to death. But before they carried out the sentence, the Christian whose boy the communists killed pleaded for the killer's life. He declared that he was young and did not know what he was doing. "Give him to me," said the father, "and I'll train him." The United Nations forces granted the request, and the father took the murderer of his son into his own home and cared for him. Today this young communist is a Christian and the Pastor of a church in South Korea.

Review and Resolve:

1. What is the relationship between sacrifice (worship) and restitution?
2. What is our responsibility to righting offenses, and does it matter who is at fault?
3. Why do you think God makes this issue such a priority?
4. Why does Jesus want this done as soon as possible?
5. What are the three results of immediate reconciliation?
6. Can you give an illustration of someone who has forgiven someone else?
7. Resolve to forgive someone this week or ask for forgiveness.

Chapter 14

The Surgical Cure

You have heard that it was said, 'You shall not commit adultery;' but I say to you, that everyone who looks on a woman to lust for her has committed adultery with her already in his heart. And if your right eye makes you stumble, tear it out, and throw it from you; for it is better for you that one of the parts of your body perish, than for your whole body to be thrown into hell. And if your right-hand makes you stumble, cut it off, and throw it from you for it is better for you that one of the parts of your body perish than for your whole body to go into hell (Matthew 5:27-30).

Just as Jesus went beyond murder to anger, now He goes beyond adultery to lust. He proclaims that it is not the action but the attitude, the inner thought, that counts the most. We must remember that sin is a matter of one's mind and heart and not just a matter of act. Our actions are merely expressions of our inward sin. And, of course, we all realize our Lord was not condemning the human moral desires God put into people. What He was condemning was the deliberate intention to lust. Martin Luther said, "We cannot keep the birds from flying over our heads, but we can keep them from building a nest in our hair."

We must remember the principle we are dealing with in this entire section of Scripture. The Pharisees were concerned only about outward obedience to the Law. They did not understand that ethics involves not only an external act but also a heart attitude. Our heart intention is the primary focus for all our ethical decisions. Therefore, good behavior is more than conformity to a set of rules. It is a condition of heart and attitude. That is what the Pharisees missed.

Jesus is revealing the heart of God to us rather than the letter of the Law. He introduces much of this discussion with the familiar phrase, *You have heard that it was said... but I say to you ...* He uses this formula six times in this chapter. In each case, He will refer to the Law or a Pharisaic addition, and then He will reveal the heart of God in the Matter. Thus, He shows us how our righteousness is to exceed the righteousness of the Scribes and Pharisees.

Here He emphasizes the importance of our inner thoughts and gives a very drastic illustration of eliminating temptation. Each of us must deal with temptation and the course of our lives may depend on how we treat it. Even the Pharisees had to deal with this problem. Among the Pharisees, was a small sect called the "Blind, Bruised, and Bleeding Pharisees." This small group got its name because they would walk around with their eyes closed. They didn't want the temptation that came with seeing anyone, especially a woman. Consequently, they were constantly bumping into walls and posts and were bruised and bleeding. This attitude infected all the Pharisees.

The New Testament Principle on Adultery (Matthew 5:27-28).

We may say that Jesus is here beginning to talk about family life. In this case, He is dealing with the sin of adultery and traces its roots to the individual's thoughts. Verse 27 refers to the seventh commandment in Exodus 20:14. He has just finished dealing with the sixth commandment in Exodus 20:13.

What is Adultery?

The word Jesus uses in this verse for adultery is the Greek word moikeuo, used thirteen times in the New Testament and four times in the book of Matthew itself. The term translates as "adultery" or "to commit adultery." It is committing unlawful sexual intercourse with a person who is not your spouse while you are married.

Adultery and the Pharisees:

The Pharisees and the rabbis were attempting to limit the scope of the commandment *you shall not commit adultery* only to the act itself. However, the tenth commandment against covetousness includes the sin of desiring another man's wife. They found it more comfortable to ignore this truth. In their view, they and their pupils kept the seventh commandment if they avoided the act of adultery itself. As a result, they gave a relatively narrow definition of sexual sin and a conveniently broad definition of sexual purity.

However, Jesus taught differently. He extended the implications of divine prohibition. Instead, He affirmed that the true meaning of God's command was much broader than a mere prohibition of acts of sexual immorality. As the prohibition of murder included the angry thought and the insulting word, the ban on adultery had a lustful look and imagination. We can murder with our words and commit adultery with our hearts and minds.

Sin in the Heart:

In verse 28, the Lord Jesus shows our difficulty in detail. He says, in contrast to the thinking of the Pharisees, ... *everyone who looks on a woman to lust for her has committed adultery with her already in his heart.* The same principle applies when we reverse. Women lust too. Sin is both an act we do, and an attitude expressed. He steps beyond the law and puts our sin right within us where it begins and belongs. A man can sin in his mind. Temptation can come, and sin complete before carrying out the act.

I should make two points before we go any further. First, there is not the slightest suggestion here that natural sexual relations within the commitment of marriage are anything but God-given and beautiful. We may thank God that the Song of Solomon is contained in the canon of Scripture because it includes the uninhibited delight of lovers, of bride and bridegroom in each other. No, the teaching of Jesus here refers to unlawful sex outside of marriage. Also, He is not forbidding us to look at a woman, but that we do not do it lustfully. We all know the difference between looking and lusting. The word He uses for lust is epithumeo, which means "to set one's heart upon, to desire, lust after, and covet." When you think like that about another woman who is not your wife, you commit adultery, and do not even have to carry out the act.

The second point Jesus alludes to refers to all forms of immorality. To argue that the reference is only to a man lusting after a woman and not vice versa, or only to a married man and not an unmarried, since the offender is said to commit "adultery," not "fornication," is to be guilty of the same false interpretation of the Pharisees. He emphasizes that any and every immoral sexual practice in deed is immoral also in look and thought.

The Cure for the Sin of Adultery (Matthew 5:29-30).

When we come to verses 29-30, Jesus makes a great demand upon those listening to Him. First, he insists we eliminate anything that causes or seduces us to sin.

The word He uses for "stumble" is interesting. It is the word skandalizei and is the word from which we get our English word, "scandal or scandalize." It refers to the bait stick in a trap. The rod or arm which held the bait operated the trap to catch the animal lured to its destruction. So, the word came to mean anything which causes a man's destruction.

Behind it, there are two pictures. First, there is the picture of a hidden stone in a path against which a man may stumble, or a cord stretched across a way, deliberately put there to make a man trip or of a cord stretched across a way, deliberately put there to make a man trip.

Second, there is the picture of a pit dug in the ground and deceptively covered with a thin layer of branches or of turf, and so arranged that when the unwary traveler sets his foot on it, he immediately falls into the pit. What Jesus refers to here in verse 29 is something that trips a man up, sends him crashing into destruction, and lures him to his ruin.

Figurative Language:

Of course, the words of Jesus are not to be taken with crude literalism. His words mean we must do anything that ruthlessly helps root seduction out of our lives. Suppose there is a habit that can be a seduction to sin, an association that can cause sin or pleasure that could be our ruin. In that case, that thing must be surgically removed. On the surface, it is a startling command to pluck out an offending eye, to cut off an offending hand or foot. Unfortunately, a few Christians, whose zeal greatly exceeded their wisdom, have taken Jesus' words literally enough to mutilate themselves. Perhaps the best-known example is the third-century scholar Origen of Alexandria. He went to extremes of asceticism, renouncing possessions, food, and even sleep. In an over-literal interpretation of this passage and of Matthew 19:12, he made himself a eunuch. Not long after, in A.D. 325, the Council of Nicea was right to forbid this barbaric practice, and discontinued it.

The command to get rid of troublesome eyes, hands, and feet exemplifies our Lord's use of dramatic figures of speech. He was advocating not literal physical self-maiming but ruthless moral self-denial. It is not mutilation but mortification that is the path to holiness. He taught mortification, or taking up the cross to follow Christ, was a means to reject sinful practices so firmly that we die to them and put them to death.

The Need for Surgery:

Why is it necessary to be so radical in this process? The answer is that it will save us from ultimate judgment. Notice the end of both verses 29 and 30: *For it is better for you that one of the parts of your body perish, than for your whole body to be thrown into hell.* These words of Jesus indicate that the inconvenience is worth it compared to the ultimate consequences, such as falling under God's wrath. The word Jesus uses for hell is Gehenna, which refers to the valley of lamentation and the site southwest of Jerusalem that we spoke of earlier in this study. The name became a symbol of the place of future punishment. That is how the New Testament uses this word.

This passage may refer to eternal judgment or the certainty of judgment in this life. Whatever the case, the cost is high! So, nothing is too precious to eliminate from your life if it will cause your heart to lust and, ultimately, affect your eternal destiny. In other words, losing a part is better than losing the whole. This warning is a great deterrent to those not always motivated by our love for God and others. We will feel the judgment of God if we don't heed this instruction.

Conclusion:

If we do not eliminate the desire for adultery, we quickly begin to make excuses for the act of adultery. I have heard the following classics over the years to explain away sexual sin. Of course, we would expect these statements from non-Christians, but we also note them from Christians. You will notice a few of them even have a spiritual touch.

1. "We are in love, so how can it be wrong? We are consenting adults." The sinner does not decide what violates the rules. Only God does that (Ephesians 5:3-7).
2. "We are not hurting anyone else." Contrarily, you hurt yourself, another person, and your entire future (I Corinthians 6:15-20).
3. "God will forgive; it's not a big deal" (1 Corinthians 6:9-11).
4. "We are engaged, so it doesn't matter." Many engagements don't end in marriage. If they do, the scars of mistrust and hurt stay with you after marriage. If you cannot control yourself before marriage, don't be deceived into thinking you will suddenly be self-controlled after marriage. 1 Corinthians 7:9, 36 gives special instructions to couples who are Christians and struggling with passion.
5. "My divorce isn't final. As soon as it is, we'll get married."
6. "I need someone, that's why we sleep together" (1 Corinthians 7:9).
7. "We live together until we see if we can make it" (Hebrews 13:4).
8. "I don't believe in fornication and adultery, but sex with meaning is okay. I see it as God's way of releasing tensions." That is double-talk for fornication.
9. "We have a spiritual marriage in the eyes of God. We just haven't made it legal." Remember anything not made legal is illegal. Marriage is both legal and spiritual in God's eyes. A public witness is necessary for leaving and cleaving. This excuse is a cover for lack of commitment and sin in God's eyes.

God accepts no excuse for sexual immorality. If an attitude of immorality is sin, the act is likewise sin. Once we know we sin in our hearts before the action, we will be cautious about the meditation of our hearts. Therefore, let me ask you to take inventory of your heart. What have you been meditating on lately? If the result of that meditation is breaking of one of God's laws, then that meditation is sin. If you desire to sin, you already have. If you continue lusting and commit the act, you will have sinned twice, and the consequences will be much greater than if you stopped and repented.

What is your fantasy? Jesus calls us to purity of heart, so we can see God and others can see God through us. So, what is the answer? The answer to this kind of sin in the mind or heart is not repression or expression but substitution. Philippians 4:8 gives the acceptable substitution:

> *Finally, brothers,*
> *whatever is true,*
> *whatever is noble,*
> *whatever is right,*
> *whatever is pure,*
> *whatever is lovely,*
> *whatever is admirable,*
> *if anything is excellent or praiseworthy,*
> *think about such things.*

If you think the worst about someone (anger or lust), replace those thoughts with what you know is true and of good report.

Review and Resolve:

1. How do you feel about the basic principle in this lesson, "Ethics involves not only an external act, but also a heart attitude?"
2. Define "adultery."
3. What was the difference between how the Pharisees looked at adultery and how Jesus looked at it?
4. What does Jesus mean when He uses this figurative language?
5. What is the best way to keep your mind right?
6. What other excuses have you heard to justify sexual immorality?

Chapter 15

The Bond We Must Not Break

And it was said, 'Whoever divorces his wife, let him give her a certificate of dismissal;' but I say to you that everyone who divorces his wife, except for the cause of unchastity, makes her commit adultery; and whoever marries a divorced woman commits adultery. (Matthew 5:31-32)

I don't think I need to tell you how serious the matter of divorce is, not only in our country but worldwide. In many communities today, divorces are more frequent than marriages. It is affecting all of us. It has been many years since several states published statistics showing that child abuse is at an all-time high because of the number of stepparents involved in the children's lives.

Divorce has been an issue among Christians for as long as Christianity has existed. However, over twenty years ago, society began to experience this problem's results. In "USA Today," in 1983, the story of one child in a child guidance clinic showed the need in society and culture.

"Four-year-old Joshua grabs a toy house, then picks up three paper dolls, mom, dad, and child. He smashes the house hard on top of all of them. 'The whole family is crushed,' Joshua says softly, his big green eyes looking sober and sad. More action comes quickly at the Los Angeles San Fernando Valley Child Guidance Clinic. Plastic parent snakes slither off, leaving their baby behind to starve, or so the preschoolers say. Mom dolls burn to death and daddy puppets are thrown into the trash because, it's claimed, they've killed their kids.

"However bizarre their fantasies, Joshua and his playmates are normal, for kids with divorcing parents. When couples in the USA divorce, they've been married an average of six years (and the time has become much shorter from 2008 to the present). Demographers report, "One child in four lives through a divorce before age seven, and that number is likely to reach fifty percent within a few years,"

The divorce rate has risen 700% in the twentieth century and continues to increase. The U.S. Census Bureau gave the following figures:

> In 1920 there was 1 divorce for every 7 marriages.
> 1940, 1 divorce for every 6 marriages.
> 1960, 1 divorce for every 4 marriages.
> 1972, 1 divorce for every 3 marriages.
> 1977, 1 divorce for every 1.8 marriages.

The divorce rate has recently dropped, but fewer people are also getting married. According to the US Census Bureau, April 22, 2021, between 2008 and 2016, the median age at first marriage rose approximately two full years to 30 for men and 28 for women.

Among ever-married adults 20 years and over, 34% of women and 33% of men had ever been divorced; the percentage ever-divorced was highest (about 43%) for adults of both sexes, ages 55 to 64.

Now, the entire family unit, as we know it, has been dispensed. By 2000, in many states, there were more divorces yearly than marriages. Over one million children a year are involved in divorce cases, and thirteen million under 18 now have one or both parents missing. We, as Christians, need to know how we can be more effective in ministering to many ensnared in this circumstance. We must also know understand how to prevent others, including ourselves, from getting caught up in the same trap.

Even worse, our culture has changed many of the rules regarding sex and marriage. For example, in October 2008, a school administrator in San Francisco required the first-grade class of his school to attend and even participate in a gay marriage for education (indoctrination). One of the women getting married was their first-grade teacher. The gay mayor of San Francisco gladly performed the marriage. Only two parents in the class protested that the administration forced their children to attend and participate in this marriage. By 2020, they openly taught children about sex changes, and many participated without parental knowledge.

The problem is that, for the most part, the church has not adequately dealt with this entire area of life and theology. As a result, the church is confused by the culture and what is acceptable in society. Further, the issue of divorce is complicated for a pastor to address because of the diversity of circumstances present in any congregation. How can we answer every question and deal with every circumstance present? There are so many "what ifs" or "what do you do when" that people have usually decided based on subjective feelings rather than objective biblical teaching.

Where do we go for help? The best source of information on the subject is God's Word. It is essential to take our feelings out of the picture and rely only on a raw, objective interpretation of the Word of God on the issue. My purpose is to shed some light on the passage before us but not to deal with every passage on the subject. We will, however, talk about a few other passages in God's Word. Our problem in the church is that many Christians have not bothered to read the Bible on this subject. They may have gotten their understanding of divorce and remarriage by osmosis from other people who have not read the Bible, society, or their experience. Interestingly, when we finally read the Bible, it says much less than we assumed. We must stop relying on the writings of others and go to the text for ourselves and see what God says on this critical subject.

The Significance of This Passage:

Looking at Matthew 5:32 and Matthew 19:9, you realize these passages are significant in this discussion of divorce and remarriage. The actual reason is that one will interpret all the other Biblical evidence based on how he interprets these passages. For example, suppose you approach I Corinthians 7 with the view that Jesus gives an exception in these passages. In that case, it will determine how you interpret I Corinthians 7. We can say the same of Deuteronomy 24 and the book of Malachi as well as all other passages in the Bible which deal with the subject. As we have already said, the Bible does not say a lot on this subject, but what it does say will be determined by the reader according to how he interprets these verses.

That is why we must decide just what these verses mean. Then, once we have come to a proper and correct conclusion, we will have an appropriate interpretation of the other passages.

The Present, Acceptable View:

It seems to me that the entire issue hinges on how we view the "exception clause," primarily built on the word porneia. The term used in Matthew 5:32 and in Matthew 19:9 will help us understand how this word is understood by many around us today.

Let me say that many in Christianity today view porneia to mean adultery. And we will show how that is the case:

Dr. Stanley Ellison says, "But the exception which Jesus included in both statements is just as binding and must not be overlooked. That exception is where one or both partners have involved themselves in porneia (fornication, immorality, unchastity, etc.). So what does the term mean? In the Old Testament, the equivalent term, zanah, almost universally represented adultery. The New Testament uses the term 26 times, referring to all types of illicit sexual intercourse. It is a broader term than adultery (moicheia) but often includes it. Jesus used the term porneia here rather than moicheia to show the disastrous effect of illicit sexual relations on the marriage relationship." (<u>Divorce and Remarriage in the Church</u> by Stanley A. Ellison, Zondervan. 1977).

John R.W. Stott says, "It seems, therefore, that we must agree with R.V.G. Tasker's conclusion that porneia is 'a comprehensive word, including adulter, fornication and unnatural vice.'" (<u>The Message of the Sermon on the Mount</u>, John R.W. Stott, Inter-Varsity Press).

Talking about Porneia, D.A. Carson says, "The only exception which Jesus will allow is fornication. Different Christians have said this word refers to all sorts of specific sins; but as far as I can see it is an inclusive term that refers to all sexual irregularity. For a married couple, it involves sexual marital unfaithfulness." (<u>The Sermon on the Mount</u>, A.D. Carson, Baker Book House, 1978).

Also, Guy Duty states that "Adultery is a sufficient ground for divorce because it is an actual breaking of the marriage tie." Again, he is quoting Johann Bengel (1713-1741). (<u>Divorce and Remarriage</u>, Guy Duty, Bethany Fellowship, Inc., 1967).

Referring to Matthew 19:9, John MacArthur states, "The word fornication (Gk., porneia) is commonly used to encompass adultery ... Adultery was the only thing that could break the bond of marriage." (<u>On Divorce</u>, John MacArthur, Moody Press, 1983).

In his book, Divorce, John Murry says about Matthew 5:32: "Fornication is unequivocally stated to be the only legitimate ground for which a man may put away his wife. The word used here is the more generic term for sexual uncleanness, namely, fornication.... it is, of course, implied that such on the part of a married woman is not only fornication but also adultery in the specific sense, for the simple reason that it constitutes sexual infidelity to her spouse."

The Meaning of Porneia:

I submit that the meaning of porneia is not that of adultery. However, the word can indeed mean adultery, although that is not its first meaning. It can indeed have a broad sense of meaning as well. However, at the risk of sticking my neck out, I would like to give you some reasons why I think this term should take a reasonably strict meaning and cannot mean adultery in these passages. Further, I would like to show that the way the term is used in Matthew virtually demands its meaning be uniquely Jewish. Let's look at the one word that seems to form our entire theology on divorce and remarriage.

1.   **The Lexical Meaning.** First, this word's first meaning is not "adultery." After having checked many Greek Lexicons (dictionaries), I have concluded that its primary meaning is "fornication." Our first understanding of any word in the Scriptures comes from its meaning in the lexicons. That must also be our approach to understanding porneia.

Perhaps the most prestigious Greek Lexicons is Liddell and Scott's massive volume. They give the following definition of this word: "prostitution, fornication, unchastity." Not only do they give prostitution and fornication as the first meanings, but they also do not mention adultery. They also illustrate how prostitution and fornication connect with people like harlots.

The Arndt and Gengrich Lexicon tell us the word means "prostitution, unchastity, or fornication." So again, this Lexicon gives us a definition that relates to people who are not married and further contrasts the term with adultery, moicheia.

G. Abbot Smith defines the term as simply "fornication." Again, this Lexicon distinguishes porneia from moicheia.

Thayer's *Greek-English Lexicon of the New Testament* gives the meaning "fornication, prostitution and illicit sexual intercourse in general." But again, the Lexicon does not provide the meaning in any way as being specifically "adultery."

Finally, in their volume, *The Vocabulary of the Greek Testament*, Moulton and Milligan state that the meaning of porneia is "prostitution, fornication, and came to be applied to unlawful sexual intercourse generally." Again, they contrast the term with moicheia.

The term porneia can indeed mean "illicit sexual intercourse in general." But unfortunately, that meaning causes many to identify the word specifically with adultery. The reasoning is that because it may mean sexual sin in general, it must also mean adultery which must be what Jesus means in the passages before us. In my mind, that becomes a very undesirable position since the term does have definite meanings. In other words, the Greek Lexicons do not support that view.

Allow me to show you the difference between fornication (porneia) and adultery (moicheia) from Baker's Dictionary of Theology. "In its more restricted sense, fornication denotes voluntary sexual communion between an unmarried person and one of the opposite sex. In this sense, the fornicators (pornoi) are distinguished from the adulterers (moichoi) as in I Corinthians 6:9. In a wider sense, porneia signifies unlawful cohabitation of either sex with a married person."

This dictionary, however, arbitrarily says that the latter meaning is that of Matthew 5:32. In other words, because the term may have a broader meaning, that is the automatic meaning in our verse. I reject that view. That reasoning is like saying, "Because I may weigh 180 pounds, I do weigh 180 pounds." Or, "Because I am capable of driving a 1965 Jaguar, I do drive a 1965 Jaguar." My wife would love that. We could not allow that reasoning to dominate our interpretation and understanding of God's Word. If we did, we would have more problems with our theology than divorce and remarriage. Because a word in Scripture may have or is capable of a particular meaning, it does not mean that term carries that meaning. To operate on that presupposition is to put our entire interpretation process in jeopardy. We must always consider other uses of a word along with the context and etymology of that particular word.

2. **The Contrast with moicheio.** Another important reason porneia cannot mean adultery in Matthew 5:32 and 19:9 is that which is contrasted with another word that implies adultery (moicheio). When you investigate the New Testament Scriptures, you find it uses two terms in the same verse in more than one place. For instance, I Corinthians 6:9 says: *Or do you not know that the unrighteous shall not inherit the kingdom of God? Do not be deceived; neither fornicators, nor idolaters, nor adulterers, nor effeminate, not homosexuals... shall inherit the kingdom of God.*

The words "effeminate and homosexuals" both are expressions which refer to homosexuals, the first of those who allowed others to use them unnaturally, and the second to active homosexuals. Paul's warning here includes the sexual vices prevalent among the Greeks and Romans of his day. He did not want Christianity to be confused with sects that permitted such things. The fact is, it becomes undeniable from 1 Corinthians 6:9 that there is a difference between adultery on the one hand and fornication on the other.

In Hebrews 13:4, we read: *Let marriage be held in honor among all and let the marriage bed be undefiled; for fornicators and adulterers God will judge.* Again, there is a contrast between these two words. They seem to be two different things to the author of this book, and he expresses two sins using the two different words. Other passages use these two words together. First is Matthew 15:19, which says, *For out of the heart come evil thoughts, murders, adulteries, fornications, thefts, false witness, slanders.*

This verse is important, not only because it uses both words in the same verse, but because they appear in the book of Matthew, where the exception clause appears, in a book specifically written to Jews. Further, it is important that they are used by Jesus. Indeed, He knew the difference between the two words, and if he meant adultery in Matthew 5:32, why didn't he use the word for adultery?

Second, Mark 7:21 says, *For from within, out of the heart of men, proceed the evil thoughts, fornications, thefts, murders, adulteries.*

It seems to me that it is not correct to say porneia always means "adultery" when in the New Testament, both words are used together in so many places. Moreover, they are used together in four books by possibly four different authors. In light of this evidence, to say porneia in Matthew 5:32 and 19:9 automatically means "adultery" is not to consider the other related Scriptural context.

Another strong contrast to make refers to the difference between porneia and other words used for immorality and other sexual sins. For instance, in II Corinthians 12:21, we read: "*... and I may mourn over many of those who have sinned in the past and not repented of the impurity, immorality, and sensuality which they have practiced.* Here porneia is set against other sexual sins, such as impurity (akatharseia) and "sensuality" or "lacentiousness" (aselgeia). The same thing is seen in Galatians 5:19: *Now the deeds of the flesh are evident, which are: immorality, impurity, (akatharseia) sensuality (aselgeia).*

Ephesians 5:3 says, *But do not let immorality or any impurity or greed even be named among you, as is proper among the saints.*

Colossians 3:5 says, *Therefore consider the members of your earthly body as dead to immorality, impurity (adatharseia), passion (pathos), evil desire (epithumia), and greed or covetousness, which amounts to idolatry.*

I don't consider myself the most outstanding student on earth. Still, it is pretty evident that in the New Testament, porneia does not always mean adultery. Furthermore, it becomes evident to me that it does not always equate to all types of sexual immorality, despite what most of the commentaries say. There are numerous instances in the New Testament where we can show a significant contrast between porneia and adultery and porneia and sexual immorality.

Conclusion:

The first thing we have seen today is the significance of this word, porneia. How we interpret this word will determine how we interpret all the rest of the New Testament truth on this subject of divorce and remarriage.

We have looked a the current, accepted view of the Matthew passages and the word porneia. Most commentators say the word automatically equates to either "adultery" or "sexual immorality."

The third thing we have seen is the word's actual meaning in the Lexicons, which call it "prostitution" or "fornication," indicating that the person involved is not married. The lexicons do not call it adultery, although there are those times when it may mean "sexual immorality" in general.

The fourth and final thing we observed is a New Testament contrast between porneia, adultery and porneia and sexual immorality in general. So, again, there is a difference between our word and the other translations and interpretations it has received in recent years.

Review and Resolve:

1. What is the best place to get information on this complex subject of divorce and remarriage?
2. What is the difference between subjective interpretation and objective theology?
3. Why are Matthew 5:31-32 and Matthew 19:9 so important to this kind of study?
4. What is the true meaning of the word **porneia**?
5. What is wrong with this statement: **"Because I am capable of driving a 1965 Jaguar, I do drive a 1965 Jaguar?"**
6. How would correct thinking on divorce and remarriage affect our society?

Chapter 16

The Bond We Must Not Break (Part II)

And it was said, 'Whoever divorces his wife, let him give her a certificate of dismissal;' but I say to you that everyone who divorces his wife, except for the cause of unchastity, makes her commit adultery; and whoever marries a divorced woman commits adultery. (Matthew 5:31-32)

Let's review the material we already covered so we can pick up this discussion in the context of what we covered in last week's lesson. I want you to know I'm repeating this information because we need to understand this message before going on to the conclusions we draw.

The Significance of This Passage:

You will remember we said this passage is significant because how we interpret it will determine how we will analyze all other Biblical evidence on this subject.

The Present, Acceptable View:

Next, we gave the current view of the passage before us. I quoted six authors to show they interpret porneia as "adultery." Those authors included Dr. Stanley Ellisen, John R.W. Stott and John MacArthur.

The Meaning of Porneia:

Our next step was to investigate the actual meaning of porneia. If you have not already noticed, our goal has been to prove that porneia in Matthew 5:32 and 19:9 does not mean "adultery." We had set out to show that Jesus was not discussing adultery when He used this word in these verses. We tested the meaning of the word in two ways:

1. **The Lexical Meaning.** First, we looked at lexicons to see their meaning of Porneia. We pointed out that the first place we always go to find the definition of a Greek word is the Greek Lexicon (Greek Dictionary). Next, we quoted five different lexicons to demonstrate the meaning of Porneia: "fornication, prostitution, unchastity, or illicit or illegal sexual intercourse in general." Finally, we pointed out that none of the lexicons define Porneia as "adultery," and most contrast the meaning of porneia with the word for "adultery," moicheia.

An important issue was it is not necessarily true that "because a Greek word is capable of a particular meaning, it is true that it carries that meaning in a particular verse." Remember my Jaguar? We must use the entire New Testament and the passage's context to determine the word's true meaning.

2. **The Context of the New Testament.** The second thing we did to determine the meaning of porneia was to observe how the New Testament uses it. We showed four passages in the New Testament where it used porneia and moicheia in the same verse. By so doing, we observed that porneia does not always mean "adultery." It, therefore, must have some other specific meaning in these passages. That meaning is "illicit sexual intercourse committed by an unmarried person," as described by *Baker's Dictionary of Theology*.

There is also an essential contrast between **porneia** and other words in the New Testament for "illicit or illegal sexual intercourse in general." We used four other passages to show this contrast. In these verses are found five other Greek words used to indicate "general sex sin." Porneia is used in each of these verses, so it cannot always mean "general sex sin."

The Context of Matthew 5:32:

We must move on to other arguments to show that Jesus is not discussing "adultery" in this passage. But first, let's observe the context of this verse:

1.   The Immediate Context. When we refer to the immediate context, we refer to the verse itself. You will remember we have shown several passages where the New Testament uses porneia and moicheia in the same verse. We concluded that if it uses two different words in the same verse, the author is communicating two individual sins. It is vital to note that this situation exists in Matthew 5:32 and 19:9.

In these verses, Jesus talks about divorce and adultery. It seems strange that if He means a person could get divorced if their mate committed adultery, He does not use the word for adultery. After all, Jesus uses the very word He would have needed twice. If He meant adultery, he would have said adultery. Instead, He said porneia. It appears once in verse 32, and moicheia appears twice. Since the two words are used, it seems Jesus means two different things. It would be unnatural for Him to use porneia where He talks about moicheia. Even Dr. Ellisen attempts to justify why Jesus would use this word instead of moicheia. It is unnatural for Him to use the two words in the same verse to mean the same thing.

2.   The Wider Context. We must also look at the broader context of this passage by going back to verse 27 and following. Jesus confronts the issue of adultery in verse 27 and quotes the Law from Exodus 20:14. Then He proceeds to say in verse 28 that you do not have to commit the literal act of adultery, you only need to look at a woman with lust in your heart, and you have already committed the sin of adultery. What He does in verse

28 is to put every one of the Pharisees in a position of condemnation. For what man has not looked at a woman with some lust at one time or another? Therefore, every Pharisee, indeed every man, is guilty of adultery.

If Jesus means we can get divorced because of the sin of adultery, He has opened the broadest possible liberty for divorce. It seems every one of us is liable to be divorced because every one of us, at some time or another, has committed adultery. That is true of men and women alike. On the one hand, Jesus would not convince us that all of us are guilty of a particular sin and then permit divorce, on the other hand, for that sin. To say we are all guilty of adultery and then allow divorce for that sin would not mean He contradicts Himself. Still, it would defeat His entire purpose in this part of the Sermon on the Mount. Porneia cannot mean adultery. Jesus said we may get divorced in this passage if it does.

However, allow me to carry this context a step further. According to Dr. Ellisen and others, when a person commits adultery, the marriage relationship is ended. I will quote from <u>Divorce and Remarriage in the Church</u>, page 96, by Dr. Stanley A. Ellisen:

"When unfaithfulness or adultery has taken place on the part of one of the partners, however, the problem then takes on a different complexion. The tragic sin of extramarital sex is so devastating in God's eyes as to signify the death of the marriage ... Fornication (to Dr. Ellisen is the same as adultery) is the one cause Jesus recognized as legitimate grounds for divorce."

Dr. Ellisen insists that when adultery has occurred, it is the death of the marriage. Guy Duty says, "adultery is a sufficient ground for divorce because it is an actual breaking of the marriage tie." If that is true, Jesus is saying in this context that all those who have committed adultery are not married. In verse 28, He points out that almost every one of us has committed the sin of adultery. Therefore, we are not married. That cannot be what Jesus means.

The context of this passage showed when Jesus used the word "porneia," He could not have meant "adultery." Therefore, if he did, by His standard, we would have all committed adultery. We are (according to Ellisen and others) not married in the first place and even divorced.

3.   The Context of the Sermon on the Mount. One of the things we have tried to observe in this study is Jesus' method in these teachings. First, Jesus says that entering the Kingdom of God is possible only by exceeding human righteousness through the righteousness of the heart.

When it comes to external righteousness, the Pharisees excelled. It is improbable that we will ever have a superficial character greater than these men. They had the pious "walk and talk" down pat It was a science to them. They would stand and pray on the street corners for everyone to hear and see. They would not even wear false teeth on the Sabbath because it was carrying a burden. They were meticulous about giving one-tenth of their income to God. They added up the commands of the first five books of the Old Testament and found 613 commands: 248 positives and 365 negatives.

In the Sermon on the Mount, Jesus confronts this kind of external righteousness. He takes everything from the exterior to the interior to the heart.

The Pharisees said, "don't commit the act of murder."

But on the other hand, Jesus said, "If you get angry at someone, you have already committed murder."

The Pharisees said, "Don't commit the act of adultery."

Jesus said, "If you have looked at a woman with lust in your heart, you have already committed adultery.

The Pharisees said, "Be sure you do not lie and above all else, keep your word."

Jesus said, "You should not have to take oaths when you say something because everything you say should be true."

The Pharisees said, "You should practice the law of retaliation, 'an eye for an eye and a tooth for a tooth.'"

Jesus said, "Allow people to slap both cheeks, give people everything you have, and go any place they want you to go."

The Pharisees said, "Love your neighbor and hate your enemy."

Jesus said, "Anybody can love his neighbor, but you love your enemies too, even those who persecute you."

Jesus takes these Pharisees to the heart of every issue. He narrows every part of their thinking and demonstrates the nature of God with the Law of God. The Pharisees said, "When you divorce your wife, be sure you give her a certificate of divorce." Jesus said, "You have no right to divorce your wife. Only if your wife has committed porneia may you divorce her."

If porneia means "adultery" or "any kind of illicit or illegal sexual sin," Jesus would be broadening the law rather than narrowing it. He would not be making their righteousness heart righteousness; He would give them more opportunity to do what they already did. In other words, a broader interpretation of porneia would deny everything Jesus is trying to do in the Sermon on the Mount. It goes against the fundamental nature of the sermon.

Our interpretation of any text, verse, or word must fit in with the heart of the text and the author's purpose (A perfect example may be found in I Corinthians 12:31 and interpretation of "earnestly desire"). To say that porneia means "adultery" in this verse defeats the purpose of Jesus on this issue of adultery, divorce, and remarriage. Why would He go to so much trouble to bring every case to the heart and then reverse Himself on this one issue? I think not!

4.   **The Context of the Synoptics.** Matthew is the apostle writing to the Jews. He is the only writer in the Synoptic Gospels who includes this exception to the "divorce-adultery rule" (Matthew 5:32; 19:9). We think it is important to note how the other Synoptic writers give the information to the Gentiles.

Mark 10:11 says: *Whoever divorces his wife and marries another woman commits adultery against her.* Mark is writing to Romans, and they did not have a betrothal period as did the Jews.

Luke 16:18 says: *Everyone who divorces his wife and marries another commits adultery; and he who marries one who is divorced from a husband commits adultery.* But, again, Luke is writing to the Greeks, and their culture has no custom of betrothal.

Mark and Luke use all-inclusive terms for those involved in this sin of divorce and adultery. We think the Holy Spirit often places words in specific passages because He wants to communicate certain truths to certain people. That is what you have here. If it were not so, Jesus would contradict Himself in the Synoptic Gospels. Which would not just be additional information.

In one place, Jesus would say we may divorce our mates under certain circumstances. In the other place He would say we may not divorce our mates under any circumstances. Which is correct? The answer is that the Matthew passages must be considered uniquely Jewish. If a Jew commits porneia (fornication, the sexual sin of an unmarried person), they are permitted release from their betrothal.

The perfect example of this is the situation between Joseph and Mary. Before Joseph knew Mary was with child by the Holy Spirit, he wanted to put her away quietly (end the engagement, considered marriage in Jewish culture). Therefore, Jesus is saying there is only one way to end that engagement in the Jewish culture—an act of porneia, a sexual sin committed by a yet unmarried person, the very definition of fornication.

Conclusion:

We conclude then that Jesus is saying there is no reason for divorce. Porneia is fornication in the strict sense of the word, which is "sexual sin committed by an unmarried person." The term may mean "illicit or illegal sexual intercourse in general." Still, giving it that meaning in this text is unnecessary or even impractical. We have shown:

> The Lexicons deny it,
> The Contest of the New Testament denies it,
> The Context of Matthew 5:32 denies it,
> The Context of the Sermon on the Mount denies it,
> The Context of the Synoptic Gospels denies it.

Therefore, there is no Biblical exception to the divorce-adultery rule. It is, consequently, improper to, on that basis, encourage or counsel a person to get divorced. Likewise, because remarriage means adultery for someone divorced, it would be inappropriate to perform a marriage for someone divorced.

It seems it is time for Christians to take the business of divorce and remarriage very seriously and stop allowing our emotions and subjectivity to control our actions in this regard. Perhaps more important, we must stop allowing our emotions to determine our theology. Divorce is not the will of God and, as Jesus points out in Matthew 19, has never been God's will. We want to live in the will of God, so let's do so. Malachi 2:16 says, *For I hate divorce, says the LORD, the God of Israel, and him who covers his garment with wrong, says the LORD of hosts. So, take heed to your spirit that you do not deal treacherously.* Whatever you do with the Malachi passage, it clearly represents less than God's ideal for His people when a divorce occurs. No passage of Scripture condones God's people participating in divorce for any reason. The counsel of God in every problem in every marriage is to work through it and not walk out on it.

Are You Divorced?

Please realize the sin of divorce, remarriage, adultery, or whatever it may be, is no different from my sin of lust, getting angry with my wife and family, mistreating my family members, sinning with my mind, or exaggerating the truth. All our sin is forgivable, and God wants to forgive all our sin. We must love and serve one another no matter what our past sins may have been. I cannot think of a more positive note to end this part of our study.

If you are divorced, you probably think, "This Hagenbaugh guy is pretty tough." However, I trust you realize your situation does not affect my feelings about you. If you read this and take a different view, please understand I would not want this interpretation of God's Word to affect our relationship. I realize many issues may bring a person to do what they see fit at the time, and I, too, grieve over those situations. However, I want every one of you to know your situation, whatever it may be, does not or will not affect my love and appreciation for you. I always believe I should accept a person for who and what they are right now and not for what they have been in the past. If people accepted me for what I have been in the past, nobody would want me around. So, we must let bygones be bygones and continue our loving relationship and friendship as it presently stands.

Well, there you have it. It is a raw and very objective interpretation of one or two of the significant passages of Scripture about divorce and from the mouth of Jesus Himself.

Review and Resolve:

1. What is there about the immediate context of Matthew 5:32 that tells us that porneia and moicheia are two different things?
2. What is the implication if Jesus means "adultery" by using the word porneia?
3. Remembering all of us already committed adultery in our hearts, what is the implication if Ellisen is right and our marriages have ended, they are dead?
4. What is the essential principle in the Sermon on the Mount?
5. How does a broader interpretation of porneia affect this most important principle in the Sermon on the Mount?
6. How does Malachi 2:16 fit into this whole discussion?
7. How can you enjoy other people regardless of their situation?

Chapter 17

A Word is a Pledge

Again, you have heard that the ancients were told, 'You shall not make false vows, but shall, fulfill your vows to the LORD.' But I say to you, make no oath at all, either by heaven, for it is the throne of God, or by the earth, for it is the footstool of His feet, or by Jerusalem, for it is the city of the great King. Nor shall you make an oath by your head, for you cannot make one hair white or black. But let your statement be, 'Yes, yes' or 'No, no;' and anything beyond these is of evil (Matthew 5:33-37).

King of England, Henry VIII, wrote a silly book against Martin Luther, for which the Pope conferred the title "Defender of the Truth." As that tyrant appeared overjoyed at the acquisition, the Jester of the court asked the reason; and being told it was because the Pope had given him that new title, the shrewd fool replied, "My good Henry, let thee and me defend each other, and let the truth alone to defend itself."

This truth is one of the most critical issues we must cope with in our lives and societies. Benjamin Disraeli said: "Time is precious, but truth is more precious than time!" Perhaps we do not spend enough time considering the importance of truthfulness and the many ways we often are not truthful.

Dr. John A. Howard, former president of Rockford College, said: "I invite you to take a little card and put it on your mirror or display it in some prominent place where it can serve as a daily reminder. I suggest that you inscribe on that card that phrase, 'Truth is outraged by silence!'"

Have you ever noticed how many ways we have in our culture to sidestep honesty through clever manipulation of words and phrases? It has become almost a science (especially during a political season) to avoid committing oneself to what we say or using the double meaning of words to deceive people. Lying has become so commonplace in government, politics, and everyday speech that a person must look for it to avoid deception. For instance, a juvenile delinquent no longer commits vandalism; he is a souvenir hunter. One must have a dictionary to know what a person means when he admits he isn't telling the truth.

Lying is called equivocation, subterfuge, bamboozlement, humbuggery, and circumvention. My favorite is euphemistic prevarications. Today, people even challenge previously proven scientific facts. For example, some can no longer define a woman. In attempting to do so, they tell real whoppers. The question is, what can we do about all of this? It doesn't matter today whether you are a Democrat or a Republican; you cannot trust those running for office. I guess they all think the people are stupid and cannot see through the rhetoric. Usually, it comes down to voting for the one we think is telling the fewest lies.

In Matthew 5:33-37, Jesus gives us a very constructive answer. He cuts through all the verbiage and provides a concise and pointed response. This response is how He would have us function and live our lives no matter what the rest of the world or society does.

The Culture of the Pharisees.

We must always interpret Scripture in light of the cultural, historical, and geographical setting. So, ask ourselves when we get to a section like this: "What did the teaching mean to those present at the time?"

Old Testament Teaching on Oaths. When we read Matthew 5:33, we hear, *You shall not make false vows,* which means, "don't perjure yourself." In other words, do not be a liar. In the Old Testament, oaths taken in the name of the Lord were binding, and perjury was strongly condemned by Scripture (Exodus 20:7; Leviticus 19:12; Deuteronomy 19:16-19). Every oath contained an affirmation or promise and an appeal to God as the omniscient punisher of falsehoods, which makes the oath binding. Thus, phrases like *as the Lord lives* in I Samuel 14:39. David used such oaths in II Samuel 19":23 and Abraham in Genesis 14:22-23; 24:2-3. In Genesis 14:22-23, for instance, Abraham entered an oath by lifting his hand to heaven, much like we do today when asked to raise our hand in a court of law to solemnly swear we are telling the truth. What does this tell us?

It shows that the Mosaic Law permitted oaths. They were part of daily commerce, a means of entering into a binding agreement settling matters without going to court. Used as legal contracts, they mean whatever a person promised, ratified by an oath, and was obligated to fulfill.

The Pharisees and Oaths. The Pharisees shifted people's attention away from the vow and the need to keep it to the formula used in making it. They argued that the Law prohibited taking of the name of the Lord in vain or cursing using God's name. So, they created a formula saying unless the name of God was attached to the oath, they were not bound to their oaths. Therefore, they did not need to keep any oath that did not involve God's name.

The Pharisees developed elaborate ways to take an oath without meaning or being willing to keep it. In other words, many word games that go on today, also happened then. They could and would keep the oath only if they wanted to. They even listed which formulas were permissible in their falsehood. In other words, they produced the "right way to lie." They used phrases that sounded very solemn and spiritual to strengthen their word, but they were covers for deception.

A perfect example is Peter in Mark 14:7: *But he began to curse and swear, 'I do not know this man you are talking about!'* Today we would say: "On my mother's grave, I'll be there!" "Trust me, I promise!" "In the name of Ralph, I'll be there!" These are unnecessary for a person of integrity.

We should not be shocked at this. After all, the Pharisees watered down murder, adultery, and divorce. Why not oaths? Here they were setting aside the spirit of the law and the letter of the law. So, Jesus directly addressed this sidestepping of the truth. It was not right then, and it is not right now.

The Correction Which Jesus Gives.

When Jesus begins to teach them in verse 34, He shows some of the substitute phrases for God they used to reinforce their word. We will notice Jesus counteracts their formula. He says, "No matter how hard you try to avoid some references to God, the whole world is His and you cannot eliminate Him from any of it. You can't therefore, eliminate God from your oath, no matter what you say."

Make no oath by Heaven. First, they cannot say, "I swear by heaven that I'll see you on Wednesday night for Bible Study and Prayer Meeting." Heaven does not leave God out because heaven is *the throne of God.* Jesus points out that heaven is the residence of God, and when they swear by heaven, they swear by the very place God lived. So, they were swearing by God anyway, even though they tried not to do so.

Make no oath by earth. They could not say, "By the power of the good earth, I will complete that project for our next Sunday School class." Jesus clarifies that they could not eliminate God from that oath because the earth *is the footstool of His feet.* The world is His footstool, and you Pharisees live on the planet, so how can you escape or eliminate God by swearing by the earth?. Of course, you cannot!

Make no oath by Jerusalem. You cannot say, "I swear by Jerusalem that I will be faithful over the next year in my giving to God's work." Jerusalem is not only the city of God; but *the city of the Great King,* the Lord Jesus Himself. They must have known He was talking about the coming Messiah who would one day rule from Jerusalem. So, again, how can God be eliminated from an oath like that?

"Make no oath by your head." Perhaps the one thing we think we can control is our bodies. But we can't say, "I swear by my head to meet you at the church's front door Sunday morning." We do not even have control over what color hair will be on our heads, so how can we think we have control over anything that happens with our bodies? Our experience with sickness and tragedy within the body of Christ here tells us that. God created us, our heads, and hair color, so how do we think we could eliminate Him from an oath like that? Impossible!

To sum it all up, the Pharisees couldn't exclude God in their use of heaven, earth, Jerusalem, or their heads, because God is in and part of everything. So, the precise wording of a vow is irrelevant, for the formula does not add to the solemnity of the vow. A vow is binding, regardless of a formula that leaves out the name of God.

The Counsel Which Jesus Gives.

In verse 37, Jesus answers the entire situation. Kingdom people must be truthful and honest all the time. We must keep our promises and be people of our word. Oaths, therefore, are not needed for kingdom people. Why? Because we give oaths to strengthen the fact that we are telling the truth. For example, we say things like, "Scout's honor," "Cross my heart," or "I promise, trust me." In most cases, these are ways of saying, "I'm telling the truth this time." Or "I lied before, but now I'm telling you the truth."

As kingdom people, we do not need to reinforce our words with a vow. When we say "Yes," it is "Yes," that's what we mean, and it is true. When we say "No," it is "No," that's what we mean, and it is always the truth. We should point out that the repetition in verse 37 emphasizes the positive and negative assertions and denial. We must remember that our word reflects our heart and what we think. It is the reflection of our character, and character does count. It is everything. Listen to what Dwight Pentecost says about this passage:

> "What we discover in this passage is that, while the Old Testament allowed oaths to legalize a pledge between two men, oaths had become necessary because men were such deceivers and liars. What was begun as a legal contract now had become absolutely necessary because of duplicity, because of the lack of regard for truth. No man's word was considered true; all men were deemed to be lying.

> "Since Christ allowed Himself to be put under oath (Matthew 26:63-64), we conclude He was not here saying, 'Do not consent to be put under an oath.' He was saying, 'Let your character, your reputation for honesty, your word be so obviously true and undefiled and without duplicity, that no man would think it necessary to put you under an oath because he suspects you of deception.' Instead of the duplicity, 'let your communication be Yes, Yes; No, No.'"

A Note on Profanity. I should say one more thing about this. Profanity is never pleasing to God. In the Kingdom of God, there is no need to reinforce or emphasize our words with profanity. We do not need additional expletives to support our speech in our conversations. When we use such language, we display a fundamental flaw in our heart of dishonesty. So, our words reveal what is in our hearts (Matthew 12:33-37). Furthermore, if we use profanity or deceit, we also need to know Satan is using us. We become a tool in his hands: *Anything beyond this comes from the evil one* (Matthew 5:37b).

Applying the Command. We need to get as practical as we can in using this command. Here are some principles we should live by as the result of what Jesus has said.

1. If you say you will do something, you had better do it. Your yes is yes in this case. (If you say you will help someone move, do it).
2. If you say you will be at a specific place, be there! (I will come over Saturday afternoon and help you with your car).
3. If you say you will be somewhere at a particular time, you better be there then.
4. If you say you will finish a job, finish it! (As God enables me, I will give the building fund a one-time or monthly). God has enabled some, and they spent the blessing on themselves. The problem with working in the Kingdom of God is not getting people to start but getting them to finish. That is the difference between a good worker and a bad one. It is true in business and the church as well.
5. If I say I will have something done at a specific time, you should be able to rest because I will do it.

Conclusion.

1. **Truth is absolute.** No degrees of truthfulness or half-truths exist. It is a whole lie. There is no such thing as a white lie. It is as black as the hell that spawned it.
2. **No separation** of secular and sacred compartments for sin exist in a disciple's life. God is everywhere and always present.
3. **Evasion of promised obligations** or undertaking using a second-class oath is unworthy of a citizen of the kingdom.

4. **Ordinary conversation** of the disciple, as well as the formal undertakings are simple and unsophisticated. His "yes" and "no," his simple promise, is to him as inviolable as the most sacred oath.

5. **The character of the disciple** is such that oaths are superfluous. His word is his bond, and others know it. Such fidelity to truth is a Christian characteristic.

6. **Jesus lifted all conversations** to the level of sacredness of an oath. The integrity of speech is to be absolute. Social evasions, conventional suppressions, ego-boosting exaggerations, insincerity in promises, and flippancy in sacred things have no place in the Christian's vocabulary.

7. **Obedience** to the Master's injunction will mark the disciple as unmistakably not of his world!

Augustine said, "When regard for truth has been broken down or even slightly weakened, all things will remain doubtful. One never errs more safely than when one errs by too much loving the truth."

Review and Resolve:

1. Give an example of someone sidestepping honesty by manipulating words or phrases.
2. How did the Mosaic Law relate to this issue of making oaths?
3. How did the Pharisees avoid using the name of God when making oaths?
4. Give a few of the corrections that Jesus made.
5. What counsel does Jesus give us in this passage?
6. How do you feel about this lesson's principle number 6 (page 113) in this lesson?

Chapter 18

The Second Mile

You have heard that it was said, 'An eye for an eye, and a tooth for a tooth.' But I say to you do not resist him who is evil; but whoever slaps you on your right cheek, turn to him the other also. And if anyone wants to sue you, and take your shirt, let him have your coat also. And whoever shall force you to go one mile, go with him two. Give to him who asks of you, and do not turn away from him who wants to borrow from you (Matthew 5:38-42).

Once there were three young marines stationed in the Orient who shared a small house. The house came complete with a Chinese houseboy named Kim. Kim was one of those patient Orientals who remained unruffled no matter what anyone did. He always seemed happy.

You know how it is, being around someone continuously cheerful; it could get to you after a while. Well, it did wear on these three marines. So, they set out to try and get Kim to lose his cool. One morning, as Kim walked into the kitchen, he opened the door, and a bucket of water fell on his head. How did Kim respond? He never missed a beat but walked over to the stove, whistling, and proceeded to cook breakfast. Another endeavor was to rub black shoe polish all over Kim's pot handles. After discovering his blackened hands, Kim wiped them clean and served soup, his smile never fading.

The pranks continued and worsened. When they nailed Kim's shoes to the floor, he tripped as he tried to walk. But, after picking himself up, he calmly got his hammer and pulled the nails out without a word. Finally, the marines had enough. With heads hanging low, they went to Kim and apologized. "Kim, we've got to apologize for what we've been doing to you. We must admit you beat us. We've never seen such a patient, forgiving man as you."

"You mean you no more put water over kitchen door?'
They answered, "No more, Kim."
"You mean you no more put black on kitchen pots?"
"No, Kim, it's over for us!"
"You mean you no more nail Kim's slippers to the floor?"
"Nope, we are really sorry, Kim, for what we've done to you."
"Okay, you be nice, and I no more spit in your soup!"

It's all too common to retaliate when someone violates our rights. We may not spit in someone's soup, but we all participate in subtle and obvious forms of retaliation. The Pharisees were so bent on revenge that they side-stepped the clear teaching of the law, took the administration of justice out of the courts, and into their own hands. They saw it as a matter of right and duty to personally take an eye for an eye and a tooth for a tooth. Here in the Lord's fifth illustration of the heart of God contrasting the law of God, we see Him dealing with unconditional love. Some have called this "The hard saying," and so it is because it goes against the very nature of our beings.

The Background of the Law:

The Law Jesus states is straight out of the Law of Moses. We see that in Exodus 21:22-29, Leviticus 24:19-20 and Deuteronomy 19:15-21. We find statements like *Life for life, eye for eye, tooth for tooth, and hand for hand, foot for foot, barn for barn, wound for wound, bruise for bruise* (Exodus 21:23-25). This law was part of the civil and moral code given to the nation to live by. It was a guide for personal moral behavior and the law of the land. Therefore, its scope covered individual circumstances and the nation's laws.

The Purpose of the Law:

The purpose of these laws was to control the chaos. Moses designated laws and ordinances to maintain and even regulate a chaotic world, giving it a certain amount of order. Can you imagine what kind of world we would live in without any moral law to control our actions?

The God of grace is also the God of Law! God will ultimately destroy evil and sin and all of its works entirely. Praise Him for that! However, He is controlling it and setting a boundary in the meantime. In other words, sin has its limits, and God has placed them.

Perhaps the second reason for the law is to create equity. God gave these laws so there would be justice. The law set limits on behavior and established punishment for behavior that breaks the law. It states the boundaries for our lives and says, "If you operate within them, you will be enormously happy. If you step out of these protective boundaries, you will be punished."

Equity in verse 38 says, *An eye for an eye and a tooth for a tooth.* If someone knocked out a man's tooth, justice demanded the courts provide equal punishment and compensation with equitable repayment for victim losses, and fair punishment for the guilty.

The third purpose of the law was to check revenge. Therefore, the principles of justice must not only see fair treatment given to the victim, but also that punishment is never excessive in its demands.

The Dispensers of Justice:

Who were the dispensers of justice? That is stated in Deuteronomy 19:17: *Then both the men who have the dispute shall stand before the LORD, before the priests and the judges who will be in office in those days.* The law in verse 38 was not to the individual but to the judges. They were responsible for law and order.

The Perversion of the Law:

The Pharisees, as usual, had taken the law and perverted it. They bent it to fit their own ends. They ignored that this teaching was for judges only and made the law in verse 38 a matter for personal application. They saw the law in their typical legalistic manner and a matter of right and duty to personally take an eye for an eye and a tooth for a tooth. They would personally carry out this law and throw restraint to the wind (Leviticus 19:18).

The Teaching of Jesus:

As is always the case in these passages, Jesus contrasts His teaching with that of the Pharisees. He puts the heart of God in contrast with that of the Pharisees. In the process, He gives a principle and then offers four mini-illustrations to apply the basic principle. The principle is, do not resist evil people! Jesus says we should not resist *"him who is evil."* This statement does not refer to Satan. Instead, it is speaking of the person who wrongs us in some way or another. When Jesus says we are not to "resist" him, He uses a word that means "to oppose, withstand, or set ourselves against." In other words, we are not to retaliate as believers.

Remember, Jesus is talking to believers. He does not say justice is unwarranted but we should leave it to law enforcement agencies. Here He is speaking to believers who have some evidence of the Beatitudes in their lives. They are the target of this instruction. The poor in spirit, the meek, the merciful, the pure, the peacemakers, etc. People who demonstrate that kind of character would not retaliate in revenge against those who wrong them.

Notice that these verses have to do with a Christian's personal relationships and not his relationships as a citizen of the country. Our relationship with our nation must consider God's whole counsel. This passage does not address our attitude toward government action, capital punishment, and pacifism. Jesus refers to personal relationships and His four examples bear that out.

We Christians must forego retaliation. It is the right we believe we possess, but Jesus here strips it from us. It is hard teaching for us because our tendency to insist on our rights lies deep in our hearts, especially as Americans. We believe in fair play. So strong is our sense of it that we naturally tend to justify retaliation as "evening the score" or "giving the other man what he deserves." Instead of insisting on our rights, we are to yield them up, particularly our imagined right to retaliation, so that preaching the Gospel might not be hindered. Of course, others will abuse and often persecute us, but we should not fight back. Paul talked about that in Romans 12:19-21.

Perhaps some of you object to this teaching. "That sounds good on paper, but we can't do it, not in the world we live in. Those words are meant for heaven." Nonsense! We *can* do it. People *are* doing it. What is more, if you are not doing it, you are not living the extraordinary, Christ-like life that God has set before you.

One illustration is Tom Skinner. The black evangelist was converted to Christ while he was the leader of the largest, toughest teenage gang in New York City, the Harlem Lords. His conversion was so genuine that he left the gang the next day, turning from a life of fighting and violence to preaching the Gospel. There was an immediate victory over crime and cruelty. Soon there was a victory over hate and bigotry also. Several weeks after his conversion, he was playing football and assigned to block the defensive end while his own halfback scored a touchdown. As he got up from the ground to head back to the huddle, the boy he had blocked jumped in front of him in a rage and slammed him in the stomach. Then, he was hacked across the back as he bent over from the blow. When Skinner fell, the boy kicked him, shouting racial slurs, and said, "I'll teach you a thing or two!"

Skinner said that under normal circumstances, the old Tom Skinner would have jumped up from the ground and pulverized the white boy. But, instead, he got up, looked the boy in the face and said, "You know, because of Jesus Christ, I love you anyway." Later, Skinner said that he even surprised himself but knew what the Bible promised was true. He was a new creature in Christ, and it was no longer necessary for him to operate on the old level of tit for tat, hate for hate, or retaliation. Moreover, the opposing end had time to think when the game was over.

He came to Skinner and said, "Tom, you've done more to knock prejudice out of me by telling me that you love me than you would have if you'd cleaned my clock."

Do not say we cannot follow the teachings of the Lord Jesus. If Christ lives in you, you can. What is more, we must follow them. If you are serious about them, why not begin by yielding to Christ's words about retaliation?

Yielding Up Our Rights:

How far should we go in giving up our rights, especially the right to retaliation? Jesus offers four illustrations to show the lengths He calls us to go. These are snapshots of different life situations.

Personal Rights: First, we must be willing to sacrifice our personal rights on the altar. Verse 39 speaks of gross insult, a sharp backhand slap to the cheek. The follower of Jesus must prepare to take another one rather than retaliate. This attitude is critical when violence and abuse arise because of our stand for righteousness (5:10-12). Still, we need not restrict the text to that.

Legal Rights: The second example concerns a lawsuit in which a man will likely lose his "shirt" (tunic), a long garment corresponding to a modern dress or suit. The follower of Jesus will also throw in the outer coat, even though Jewish law recognized this latter garment as an inalienable possession (Exodus 22:26ff). It is unlikely, of course, that people would bring a lawsuit over a suit of clothes. But a principle is at stake: we must prepare to abandon even things we regard as our legal rights. In another context, Paul enlarges on this principle when he insists that followers of Jesus will prefer to be wronged rather than to enter litigation with another follower of Jesus (I Corinthians 6:7f).

Civil Rights: Jesus probably refers to the Roman practice of commandeering civilians. An ordinary Roman soldier could legally abduct a civilian to help him, for example, to carry his luggage for a prescribed distance. Jesus' followers are not to retaliate in such cases. They are not to feel personally insulted but are to double the distance and accept the imposition cheerfully.

Property Rights: Jesus' last example demands giving and lending that is cheerful and willing. The issue is not the wisdom or foolishness of lending money to anyone who comes along (Note Proverbs 11:15; 17:18; 22:26). The burden of the passage is this: Christ will not tolerate a mercenary, tight-fisted, penny-pinching attitude which is the financial counterpart of a legalistic understanding of *an eye for an eye and a tooth for a tooth.* Don't ask yourself all the time, "What's in it for me? What can I get out of it?"

Conclusion:

The point is that retaliation is not an action for Christians. Instead, the attitude Jesus advocates is one of love, the selfless love of a person who, when injured, refuses to satisfy himself by taking revenge. The kingdom person described in the Beatitudes seeks, instead, the highest welfare of the other person and society. Based on that attitude, he determines his reaction.

What will we do? Will we hit back, returning evil for evil? First, we must allow ourselves freedom from personal animosity. Seek good, not evil. Give all we have: our clothing, service, goods, and money, for the glory of the Lord and His gospel. The only limit is that which love will impose.

Three buddies were drinking in a bar until closing time. Then, one of them said to his friends, "Hey guys, I'll bet you $20 apiece that if we go over to my house right now, I can get my wife to wake up and make us some breakfast, and she'll do it, without a word of complaint."

Without hesitation, the two responded, "You're on!"

As they entered the front door, the host drunkenly yelled, "Hey Susie, wake up, we have company, so get up and make us some breakfast." Well, the other two gazed in disbelief as Susie began preparing a full meal for the three men, even smiling as she worked.

When the breakfast was served, the bets collected, one man went to her and said, "I can't believe what I just saw. How could you possibly keep smiling when your husband treats you so rudely?"

Susie answered, "I'm a Christian and I know that one day I'll be in heaven and receive an eternal reward. I'll be happy forever. My husband, however, is not a Christian. One day he too, is going to die, but things will not be good for him. He will be suffering for eternity. So, I'm committed to making this short time he has, just as pleasant as I possibly can!" Susie's husband accepted Christ as His Lord and Savior within three weeks.

In his book *Mere Christianity*, C.S. Lewis wrote, "Do not waste your time bothering whether you 'love' your neighbor act as if you did. As soon as we do this, we find one of the great secrets. When you are behaving as if you loved someone, you will presently come to love him. If you injure someone you dislike, you will find yourself disliking him more. If you do him a good turn, you will find yourself disliking him less."

Review and Resolve:

1. What was the significance of the law as given in Exodus 21:23-25?
2. Please give the three reasons for the law as discussed in this lesson.
3. In what way did the Pharisees pervert the law?
4. What does Jesus mean when He says, *do not resist him who is evil?*
5. What is the key to being able to follow Christ's instruction in this passage?
6. Name the four kinds of Rights Jesus discusses in this passage.

Chapter 19

Loving an Irregular Person

You have heard that it was said, 'You shall love your neighbor, and hate your enemy.' But I say to you, love your enemies, and pray for those who persecute you in order that you may be sons of your Father who is in heaven; for He causes His sun to rise on the evil and the good, and sends rain on the righteous and the unrighteous. For if you love those who love you, what reward have you? Do not even the tax-gatherers do the same? And if you greet your brothers only, what do you do more than others? Therefore, you are to be perfect, as your heavenly Father is perfect (Matthew 5:43-48).

Someone said, "The Bible tells us to love our neighbors and also to love our enemies; probably because they are generally the same people!" Loving our enemies is one of the most challenging things we must do. But, again, it goes against the grain of our nature, and we must have that nature changed and replaced to accomplish this command of Scripture.

Corrie ten Boom's book, *The Hiding Place*, records one of the most moving and honest accounts of love for an enemy. Many have read her story and have wondered what compelled Corrie to as she did toward one who had caused so much pain and harm in her life.

As you read the following incident, see if you can identify with her struggle, as well as her desire to love a former enemy: "It was at a church service in Munich that I saw him, the former S.S. man who had stood guard at the shower room door in the processing center at Ravensbruck. He was the first of our actual jailers that I had seen since that time. And suddenly, it was all there, the room full of mocking men, the heaps of clothing, Betsie's pain-blanched face.

"He came up to me as the church was emptying, beaming and bowing. 'How grateful I am for your message, Fraulein.' he said. 'To think that, as you say, He has washed my sins away!'

"His hand was thrust out to shake mine. And I, who had preached so often to the people in Bloemendall the need to forgive, kept my hand at my side.

"Even as the angry, vengeful thoughts boiled through me, I saw the sin of them. Jesus Christ had died for this man; was I going to ask for more? Lord Jesus, I prayed, forgive me and help me to forgive him.

"I tried to smile, I struggled to raise my hand. I could not. I felt nothing, not the slightest spark of warmth or charity. And so again I breathed a slight prayer. 'Jesus, I cannot forgive him. Give me your forgiveness.' As I took his hand the most incredible thing happened. From my shoulder along my arm and through my hand a current seemed to pass from me to him, while into my heart sprang a love for this stranger that almost overwhelmed me. And so, I discovered that it was not our forgiveness, any more than our goodness that the world's healing hinges, but His. When He tells us to love our enemies, he gives, along with the command, the love itself." (Corrie ten Boom, *The Hiding Place*, page 238).

What compelled her to act as she did? We find the answer in the passage before us. The very struggle she had in obeying this passage is also the struggle many of us grapple with. Many of us have been in her place! Let's look at the passage:

The Old Testament Provision:

As usual, Jesus states we must deal with the Old Testament law in verse 43: *You shall love your neighbor and hate your enemy.* He is referring to Leviticus 19:18. The question is, did the law say that? Where did the Pharisees get such thoughts? The Jews, as usual, had perverted what the Old Testament law stated. Let's see how.

Their Belief. What had happened is that the teachers of the law had concluded that since the law said they were to love their neighbor, they were at liberty to hate their enemies. As you can see from the passage, they based their belief on silence.

Their Error. No place in the law states a person is free to hate his enemy. Proverbs 25:21 says, *If your enemy is hungry, give him food to eat; if he is thirsty, give him water to drink.* Romans 12:23 quotes this passage. There were incidents when the courts carried out an eye for an eye and a tooth for a tooth and times when God ordered His people to rid Israel of an enemy that was unrepentant and contaminating the land or restricting the plan of God. However, this was the judgment of God to take place under His direction. He never based His judgment on hate for people, only on the justice and judgment of God. Therefore, the Pharisees were not to take this judicial principle and put it into operation in their personal lives against their enemies. God alone reserves this right. It is still His place to judge the repentant sinner! Therefore, the Jews were twisting again, the intention of Scripture.

Who is My Neighbor? When asked this question, Jesus gave His listeners the story of the Good Samaritan (Luke 10:29-37). He expanded the concept of neighbor to mean, "My neighbor is any person whose needs I can meet." He lifted love for neighbor far above the Jewish limitation of it to one's compatriots. My neighbor is anyone who needs my assistance, be he a friend or an enemy.

Who is My Enemy? We get the answer to this question by turning to a companion passage, Luke 6:27-28: *But I tell you who hear me; love your enemies, do good to those who hate you, bless those who curse you, pray for those who mistreat you.* In other words, our enemies are people who hate, curse, and mistreat us. Notice, our enemy is someone who feels and acts negatively toward us, not the other way around! Sometimes we get confused at that point and conclude we must treat our enemies negatively.

The New Testament Position:

Jesus gives us His teaching and the teaching of the New Testament in the following verses. He gives a positive response to what otherwise is a negative issue. Notice again the formula used in contrast to the Pharisees' teaching about the law. He does not tell us to love our neighbors. That is a settled issue. However, he does deal with our enemies because that was the perversion of truth by the Pharisees. The teaching Jesus gives here is a new one found nowhere in the Old Testament. Here is what He says should be our response to our enemies:

Love Your Enemies. The natural and easy response to our enemies is to retaliate; we have already dealt with that. The Christian response demonstrates the fruit of the Holy Spirit's control of our lives, LOVE.

The word Jesus uses here for "Love" is the Greek word AGAPE. It is that love that is without variableness and conditions. It even loves when there is no return and good reasons to discourage it. Only God can produce this love, and He expresses it in our hearts. It is not a matter of feeling but a point of action. I Corinthians 13:4-8 describes this love.

This love, therefore, is way more than emotion. It involves expressions toward the deserving and the undeserving, making it possible for the Christian to love someone who is his enemy. The most important thing is not what we feel but what we will do. To give His Son to such a shameful and agonizing death as crucifixion was the last thing God would feel like doing, but He willed to do it for our sake.

Pray for Your Enemies. Have you ever tried to pray for someone and stay mad at them at the same time? I learned this lesson long ago, and it is so helpful because sometimes I find myself hurt or angered by someone's words or actions. If I am not careful, their actions become my emotional focus. So, Jesus says, pray for them. It is amazing how this works. In most cases, God has blessed the people I have been angered by and eventually returned to right the wrong. I have also done the same. As I prayed for them, I often saw where I had been wrong.

We see the purpose of this kind of prayer in verse 45. We are to pray for the following things for our enemies:

To Be Sons of God. That does not mean loving our enemies saves us, but it does mean **"Like Father, Like Son."** People will recognize a son of God, because only someone who has walked through the Beatitude sequence and received Christ as Lord and Savior could be acting like this.

To Display God's Love in Tangible Ways. The world needs concrete evidence of those who have been changed and act like God. How does God act? The answer is given in verse 45 also. God's provision benefits both the good and the bad people. It does not discriminate. Our actions must be the same.

To Benefit and Strengthen Our Lives. First, we act like God's sons because God has called us into this action. Second, we follow Christ's steps and function as He did. Third, we will drastically lessen stress and protect our bodies from physical infirmities and disease.

The Reachable Practice:

In verses 46-47, Jesus clarifies this is a reachable goal. He does this by asking two simple questions. We find the first question in verse 46. He is saying, "Loving the lovely isn't that difficult." It takes no special grace of God to love a person who loves you. It is easy to love the loveable; even tax collectors can do that (Jews and Romans hated tax collectors and considered them low-class). Loving those who love you didn't even rate a reward in Christ's mind.

The second question is asked in verse 47 and implies we are to greet not only our brothers but also our enemies. The greeting means "to draw to one's self, to embrace, welcome, to pay respects to, to greet." In other words, we should give social graces to friends. Even the pagans do that. We are to have a righteousness that exceeds that. We should also provide social graces to our enemies. Unfortunately, we tend to avoid them.

In using these questions, Jesus shows that even the tax collectors and the pagans do these things. If they can do it, we can do it. In other words, this is a reachable goal, something we can and should accomplish for the glory of the Lord Jesus Christ.

The Restated Principle:

Be perfect as your heavenly Father is perfect (Verse 48). We ask ourselves, "What does Jesus mean by 'Perfect?'" The word is TELEIOS. Used here and in other places, it describes relative perfection (adults compared to children). The word carries the idea of maturity and completeness. A person or thing is perfect when he reaches maturity and fulfills his purpose and design. Therefore, the word does not imply perfection in the sense that there are no flaws. In this context, the word "perfect" implies that God's character is sacrificial and self-imparting love, so the disciple is to be "perfect" when he reproduces that love in word and deed. He is then mature and fulfilling the purpose for which God created him in his image. A love that only does good to its friends or greets only those it loves is not perfect. It's not mature. Therefore, deal with difficult, irregular people in the same way Jesus dealt with us. He kept loving us when we did not see Him, hear Him, speak to Him, or hold Him

Conclusion:

Let's use a simple analogy. Suppose there is a loose screw in my house, and I want to tighten and adjust it. So I go to the store and purchase a screwdriver that exactly fits the grip of my hand; it is neither too large nor too small, too rough or too smooth. I lay the screwdriver on the slot of the screw, and I find that fits precisely. I then turn the screw and fix it. In the Greek sense, especially in the New Testament sense, that screwdriver is TELEIOS because it exactly fulfilled my desired purpose.

So, then, a man will be TELEIOS if he fulfills the purpose for which God created him. For what purpose was man created? The Bible tells us in the creation record: *Let us make man in our image and after our likeness* (Genesis 1:26). Man was created to be like God. The characteristic of God is this universal benevolence, this unconquerable goodwill, this constant seeking of the highest good of every man. The significant feature of God is His love for saints and sinners alike. No matter what men do to Him, God seeks nothing but their highest good. When man reproduces God's unwearied, forgiving, sacrificial benevolence, he becomes like God. He is therefore, "perfect" in the New Testament sense of the world.

It is the whole teaching of the Bible that we only realize our manhood by becoming Godlike. The one thing which can make us like God is the love that never ceases to care for men, no matter what men do to it. We realize our manhood and enter perfection when we learn to forgive as God forgives and to love as God loves.

Review and Resolve:

1. What was the Pharisees' error when they said it was permissible to *Hate your enemy"*
2. Define who your neighbor is.
3. Define who your enemy is.
4. What is the New Testament position on your relationship to an enemy?
5. What three things should we pray for an enemy?
6. How does Jesus show this is a reachable goal?
7. How does Jesus use the word "perfect" (TELEIOS) in this passage?

Chapter 20

Right Things for the Wrong Reasons

Beware of practicing your righteousness before men to be noticed by them; otherwise, you have no reward with your Father who is in heaven. When therefore you give alms do not sound a trumpet before you as the hypocrites do in the synagogues and in the streets, that they may be honored by men. Truly I say to you, they have their reward in full. But when you give alms, do not let your left hand know what your right hand is doing that your alms may be in secret; and your Father who sees in secret will repay you (Matthew 6:1-4).

Ralph Waldo Emerson (1803-1882) was an author, philosopher, and poet. Once he said, "There is no limit to what can be accomplished if it doesn't matter who gets the credit."

It often seems the formula for success is simply putting the right people in the right jobs, sitting on the sidelines, and being a good cheerleader. Our goal, especially as Christians, should be to accomplish what God wants us to achieve and bring glory to Him. But unfortunately, our motives often get in the way because we desire to bring glory to ourselves instead. That was very true of the Jews.

The Principle Stated by Jesus:

Jesus now changes His method of teaching in this sermon. He has been teaching that God's heart contrasts the teaching of the law and the Pharisees' interpretation of the law. Jesus has used that unique formula in showing the contrast between six differing teachings: Murder, Adultery, Divorce, Honesty, Justice, and Love. Now, He turns to the religious life of the Jews and proceeds to teach the heart of God in contrast to how they practiced their religion. Then, when we come down to the bottom line, He deals with their motives for doing what they do.

To the Jew, there were three great cardinal works of religious life, three great pillars on which they based the good life, Almsgiving, Prayer, and Fasting. Jesus would not have disputed that for a moment; what troubled Him was that humans often do the finest things in life for the wrong reasons.

Someone has said, "A man who wants to lead the orchestra must turn his back on the audience." The Pharisees were the religious leaders of the Jews, but they could not turn their backs on the audience as they led the band. They wanted people to see them and their righteousness. When the Jews did their almsgiving, prayer, or fasting, they did them with the sole intention of bringing glory to the doer. As a result, they lost the essential part of their value. Likewise, a man may practice good works to win praise from men, increase his prestige, and show the world how good he is.

In verse 1, Jesus says, *Beware of practicing your righteousness before men to be noticed by them.* Jesus, having demanded of his followers nothing less than perfection (5:48), is fully aware of the human heart's propensity for self-deception and issues a strong warning. *Be perfect* (5:48) but *Be careful* (6:1). In this way, Jesus presents the principle of motive. He will give us three illustrations of how the Jews of His day did the right things for the wrong reasons.

The word Jesus used for *righteousness* is what He used in 5:6, 20. Although the term is the same, the emphasis has shifted. Previously it related to kindness, purity, honesty, and love; now, it concerns almsgiving, prayer, and fasting. Thus, Jesus moves from a Christian's moral righteousness to *religious* righteousness.

It is essential to acknowledge that according to Jesus, Christian righteousness has these two dimensions, moral and religious. Unfortunately, some speak and behave as if they imagine their primary duty as Christians lies in the sphere of religious activity, whether in public (churchgoing) or private (devotional exercises). Others have reacted so sharply against such an overemphasis on piety that they talk of religion-less Christianity. The church has become a secular city for them, and prayer is a loving encounter with their neighbor. However, there is no need to choose between piety and morality. Jesus taught that authentic Christianity includes both.

The Reward for Wrong Motives:

As Jesus saw it, there is no doubt that the wrong motives for doing a thing have a certain kind of reward. Jesus states that three times in these passages. First, in verse 2, regarding almsgiving, He says, *Truly I say to you, they have their reward in full.* He makes this statement also in verses 5 and 16. A better translation might be, *They have received payment in full.* The word He used for "reward" was the technical business and commercial word for receiving payment in full. It was the word used on receipts to show that a person had paid for something in full and no further charge was necessary.

In verse 1, He says, *otherwise you have no reward with your Father who is in heaven.* Jesus put this statement together with the concept that they have received all the rewards or payments they will get. In other words, if you give alms to demonstrate your generosity, you will get the admiration of men, but that is all you will ever get. That is your full payment. If you pray in such a way as to flaunt your piety in the face of men, you will gain the reputation of being an extremely devout man, but that is all you will ever get. That is your payment in full.

Suppose you fast, so all men know you are fasting. In that case you will become known as an extraordinarily abstemious and ascetic man, but that is all you will ever get. That is your payment in full. If your one aim is for the world's rewards, you will undoubtedly get them, but you must not look for the rewards God alone can give. And he would be a sadly short-sighted creature who grasped the rewards of time and let the rewards of eternity get away from him.

The Jews and Almsgiving:

Definition of almsgiving. Perhaps it will help us understand just what this almsgiving was all about. The word here means "mercy, pity, particularly in giving" to the poor. Moses imposed for all time the obligation, *For the poor will never cease to be in the land; therefore I command you, saying, 'you shall freely open your hand to your brother, to your needy and poor in your land* (Deuteronomy 15:11). As a result, among the Jews, they made specific provisions for the regular distribution of alms on a large scale among the poorer members of the Commonwealth, the Sabbatical year (Exodus 23:11); the gleanings of field and fruit (Leviticus 23:22); tithes laid up in store every third year for the Levite, the stranger, the fatherless, and the widow (Deuteronomy 14:28-29); the freeing at Jubilee of the poor (Leviticus 25:39-54), as well as other provisions.

The Jews ordered two collections. They distributed a daily supply of food every morning and a weekly collection of money distributed weekly. There was also a chamber in the Temple where they secretly deposited alms for the poor of good families who did not wish to receive charity openly.

Jewish Attitudes about Almsgiving. Almsgiving came to be associated with merit and was looked upon as a means of pacifying God's favor and warding off evil (Daniel 4:27) and was among the essential virtues of the godly (Isaiah 58:4-7; Ezekiel 18:7; Amos 2:7). The people regarded soliciting alms as a curse from God, and Judaism gave no encouragement to begging as a sacred calling.

To the Jew, almsgiving was the most sacred of all religious duties. How sacred it was may be seen from the fact that the Jews used the same word both for almsgiving and righteousness (tzedakah). To them, to give alms and be righteous were the same. To give alms was to gain merit in the sight of God and was even to win atonement and forgiveness for past sins. We see this in some of the Jewish writings. "It is better to give alms than to lay up gold; almsgiving doth deliver from death, and it purges away all sin" (Tobit 12:8). Also, we read in Ecclesiasticus 3:14-15: *Almsgiving to a father shall not be blotted out, and as a substitute for sins it shall stand firmly planted. In the day of affliction, it shall be remembered to your credit. It shall obliterate your iniquities as the head, the frost.* A rabbinic saying also says: "Greater is he who gives alms than he who offers all sacrifices." Job 29:23ff shows the antiquity of almsgiving. It is easy to see that almsgiving stood first in the catalog of good works for the Jews.

Jesus Rebukes the Jews. Jesus talks about not sounding a trumpet in verse 2. The Pharisees loved the praise of men, but we do not know whether they sounded a trumpet when they gave alms. However, whether Pharisees sometimes did this literally or whether Jesus was painting an amusing caricature does not matter. In either case, He was rebuking our childish attempt to be highly esteemed by men.

Spurgeon said, "To stand with a penny in one hand and a trumpet in the other is the posture of hypocrisy." That seems to be just what Jesus called the Pharisees at this point. He calls them "hypocrites." This word was first an orator and then an actor. So figuratively, the term applied to anybody who treats the world as a stage on which he plays a part. He lays aside his identity and assumes a false one. He is no longer himself, but in disguise, impersonating someone else. He wears a mask.

Now in a theater, there is no harm or deceit in actors playing their parts. It is an accepted occupation. The audience knows they have come to a drama; they are not taken in by it. But on the other hand, the trouble with the religious hypocrite is that he deliberately sets out to deceive people. He is like an actor in that he is pretending (so what we see is not the actual person but a part, a mask, a disguise). Yet, he is quite unlike the actor in this respect: he takes some religious practice which is an actual activity, and turns it into make-believe, a theatrical display before an audience. And it is all done for applause.

The Christian Way of Giving.

Secret Giving. Having forbidden His followers to give to the needy in the ostentatious manner of the Pharisees, Jesus now tells the Christian, His way of giving. In verse 3, He says we should not let our left hand know what our right hand is doing. Not only are we not to tell other people about our Christian giving, but there is also a sense in which we are not even to tell ourselves. We are not to be self-conscious in our giving, for our self-consciousness will readily deteriorate into self-righteousness. So subtle is the sinfulness of the heart that it is possible to take deliberate steps to keep our giving secret from men while simultaneously dwelling on it in the spirit of self-congratulation. Concerning verse 3, John Calvin writes, "He means that we ought to be satisfied with having God for our only witness."

The Proper Reward. So, we are to give "secretly," to protect ourselves from ostentatious pseudo-piety and to ensure that we act righteously before the Lord. Our Father who sees in secret will repay us. It is again made clear that the follower of Jesus is interested in God's blessings and rewards and not in men's transient approval.

What is the "reward" the heavenly Father gives the secret giver? It is neither public nor necessarily in the future. Nevertheless, it is probably the only reward that genuine love wants when making a gift to the needy, namely, to see the need relieved. His gifts feed the hungry, clothe the naked, heal the sick, free the oppressed, and save the lost. whereby the love that promoted the gift is satisfied. Such love (God's own life expressed through man) brings secret joys, that desire no other reward.

To sum up, our Christian giving is to be neither before men (waiting for the clapping) nor even before ourselves (our left hand applauding our right hand's generosity) but "before God," who sees our secret heart and rewards us with the discovery that, as Jesus said, *It is more blessed to give than to receive* (Acts 20:35).

Conclusion.

It is easy to poke fun at those Jewish Pharisees of the first century. Our Christian Phariseeism is not so amusing. We may not employ a troop of trumpeters to blow a fanfare each time we give to a church or charity. Yet, to use the familiar metaphor, we like to "blow our own horn." Seeing our name on charity subscribers and supporters of good causes boosts our ego. We fall to the same temptation: we draw attention to our giving to "be praised by men."

J.L. Kraft, head of the Kraft Cheese Corporation, gave approximately 25% of his enormous income to Christian causes for many years. He said, "The only investment I ever made which has paid consistently increasing dividends is the money I have given to the Lord."

J.D. Rockefeller said, "I never would have been able to tithe the first million dollars I ever made if I had not tithed my first salary, which was $1.50 per week."

Review and Resolve:

1. What is the principle of this passage, as Jesus states it?
2. What does Jesus mean when He says, *Truly I say to you, they have their reward in full?*
3. Can you ever think of a time when you did the right thing with the wrong motives?
4. How do you think that almsgiving got to the level for the Jews to forgive sin?
5. What do you think is the reward for the secret giver?
6. What other areas of Christianity do we tend to "blow our own horn?"

Chapter 21

The True Pattern for Prayer

And when you pray, you are not to be as the hypocrites; for they love to stand and pray in the synagogues and on the street corners, in order to be seen by men. Truly I say to you, they have their reward in full. But you, when you pray, go into your inner room and when you have shut the door, pray to your Father who is in secret, and your Father who sees in secret will repay you. And when you are praying, do not use meaningless repetition, as the Gentiles do, for they suppose that they will be heard for their many words. Therefore do not be like them; for your Father knows what you need, before you ask Him. Pray then, in this way: 'Our Father who art in heaven, Hallowed by Thy name. Thy Kingdom come. Thy will be done, On earth as it is in heaven. Give us this day our daily bread. And forgive us our debts, as we also have forgiven our debtors. And do not lead us into temptation, but deliver us from evil. For Thine is the kingdom, and the power, and the glory, forever. Amen.' For if you forgive men for their transgressions, your heavenly Father will also forgive you. But if you do not forgive men. Then your Father will not forgive your transgressions (Matthew 6:5-15).

ne night, a man had a dream in which he found himself in a large church with the old but faithful custodian. The custodian went around with a light through the entire church to ensure everything was in order before he locked up the place. looking into the roof's dim recesses, the man could distinguish many handsome birds hopelessly floundering about, trying to get through the roof. At the same time, some other birds lay on the beams and rafters as though they had fallen asleep but had beaten themselves to death. "What are these? What is the meaning of this?" asked the man in amazement.

"Oh," said the old custodian, "these are some prayers said today by some people. These will never reach God because they are mere words said by people who said them so others might hear. Only the heart's prayers are heard by the Father in heaven, and it seems there are very few of those."

We must realize that what we say is not as important to God as how we say it. I wonder how often our prayers are merely words to God. Jesus gave crucial instructions and told us exactly how we should pray. He first lays down a foundational principle. It is negative in form but positive in intention and result. The principle begins with the word *Beware* or *Take Heed* (KJV). It means *hold the mind on a matter.* He wants us to listen to what He has to say. We must hold our minds on this principle.

He then explains the principle for us: *Beware of practicing your righteousness* (alms, equivalent to righteous acts. The expression refers to religious externals), *before men to be noticed by them* (verse 1). This principle applies to all spirituality and specifically in almsgiving, prayer, and fasting. He tells us that people who do not obey this great principle already have their reward among men, and there is no reward with their Father, who is in heaven. It is the matter of prayer at which we want to look.

Jesus deals with the three issues from negative and positive aspects. As we consider the matter of prayer in this regard, the negative and positive form our outline.

The Negative Admonitions (Matthew 6:5-8).

Not as The Hypocrites Do. When Jesus speaks of "the hypocrites" here, He talks about the Jews, especially the Jewish religious leaders, the Pharisees. The Jews had a higher ideal of prayer than any other nation. No religion ever ranked prayer higher on the scale of priorities. To the Jews, no good work was more significant than prayer. There is a rabbinic saying: "He who prays within his house surrounds it with a wall that is stronger than iron." The only regret of the rabbis was that it was not possible to pray all day long.

But specific problems had set into the Jewish concept of prayer. The issues about which we speak are not peculiar to the Jews. They can happen anywhere. While they are not faults of neglect, they are faults of misguided devotion.

Prayer Became More and More Formalized. They had to repeat specific prayers at certain times. If the last possible moment for saying one of the prayers had come, no matter where a man found himself, at home, in the street, at work, or in the synagogue, he had to stop and say it. Some indeed loved these prayers and repeated them out of reverence, devotion, adoration, and love. However, often, people garbled their way through it and went on their way.

Jewish Liturgy Supplied Stated Prayers for All Occasions. Almost every event in life had its stated formula of prayer. There were prayers relating to meals, light, fire, lightning, new moons, comets, rain, tempest, sea, lakes, rivers, good news and bad, using new furniture, entering, and leaving a city, and of course, weddings, funerals, accidents, and scores of others. But, since the prayers were meticulously prescribed and stated, it became easy for a prayer to slip off the lips with little meaning. Only mere words!

The Jew Had Set-Times for Prayer. These times were 9 am, 12 middays, and 3 pm. Of course, it is lovely for a man to remember God three times a day, but there is a genuine danger a man might babble out a prayer that three times a day without a thought of God.

Prayer Should Connect with Certain Places, especially the synagogue. While it is true that God seems near in specific areas, we may offer prayer anywhere. Some Rabbis who went so far as to say that prayer was efficacious only if offered in the Temple or Synagogue. As a result, the Jews went to the temple at the hour of prayer. We see Peter and John doing just that in Acts 3:1. The danger is that man might think of God as confined to certain holy places. He might forget that the whole earth is the temple of God.

Jews Tended Toward Long Prayers. But, of course, history shows that tendency is not only confined to the Jews. It is also true, for instance, of the 18th-century worship in Scotland. Fr. W.D. Maxwell writes, "The efficacy of prayer was measured by its ardor and its fluency, and not least by its fervid lengthiness." It is easy to confuse verbosity with piety and fluency with devotion.

Notice what Solomon says in Ecclesiastes 5:1-2: *Guard your steps as you go to the house of God and draw near to listen rather than to offer the sacrifice of fools; for they do not know they are doing evil. Do not be hasty in word or impulsive in thought to bring up a matter in the presence of God. For God is in heaven and you are on earth, therefore let your words be few.*

Jew Used Certain Forms of Repetition. Like all eastern peoples, they used and overused these forms. The eastern peoples could hypnotize themselves by the endless repetition of one phrase or even a word. In I Kings 18:26, the prophets of Baal cried out, *O Baal hear us,* for half a day. In Acts 19:34, the Ephesian mob shouted, *Great is Diana of the Ephesians,* for two hours. Islam will repeat the sacred syllable "HE" for hours on end.

The Jews did a similar thing. They often attempted to pile up every possible title and adjective in their address to God in prayer. One famous prayer begins: "Blessed, praised, and glorified, exalted, extolled, and honored, magnified, and lauded by the name of the Holy one." There is a kind of intoxication in words. When a man begins to think more about how he is praying than what he is praying, his prayer dies upon his lips.

The Final Fault was Praying to be Seen by Men. Their system of prayer made ostentation very easy. They prayed while standing, with hands stretched out, palms upward (emptiness before God) and bowed heads. They had to pray at 9 am, 12 middays, and 3 pm. It was easy to stand on a busy street corner or in a crowded city square so the world could see their devotion. It was easy for people to admire them for their exceptional piety. They easily put on an act of prayer (a performance) for the whole world to see.

Jesus calls these people hypocrites. They loved to pray in the Synagogue because that was the place of prayer or on the street corner so men might see them do it. Their fault was that they were praying to men and not to God. Therefore, we must be less concerned with impressing the congregation and more with contacting God.

What is the answer to all of this? Secret prayer! The privacy of worship becomes an essential issue with Jesus. The inner chamber with the door shut is the proper place of prayer. Jesus does not mean that prayer must be secret, but we should not flaunt it before other people. He illustrates the inner chamber with the door shut to tell us we do not pray because other people are watching.

How much do we know about the true place of prayer? When a man announces that he is always, at such a time, in the inner room with the door shut, that is a denial of secrecy. The principle is that we go there when no one else knows. We escape from human observation to aloneness with God. That becomes the first principle of prayer.

In many senses, the plant's root is the most critical part of it. Yet, men do not see it. Instead, it hides under the ground, in the dark, where it works away, preparing the life that grows into the plant and shows itself in the trunk, branches, leaves, and fruit. So, it is in the Christian life. It is not this secret prayer that men can see. Yet, it is in the inner room with the door shut that this life grows.

Not as the Heathen Do. Jesus further refers to the repetition of the eastern peoples we have already discussed. He calls them "Gentiles," meaning unbelievers, "pagans." He is talking about babbling or chanting, which is "meaningless repetition." We have already mentioned where some of this has taken place, even in the Scriptures.

He is pointing out that heathen have a wrong concept of prayer. For one thing, they thought that they could force God into doing what they wanted Him to do. That said something about their value of prayer. They valued it as a tool to move God into performance. However, they also misused prayer to change God's mind. They had the misconception that if prayer was long enough, often enough, and with enough repetition it would change God's mind to meet their desires.

The procedure's folly is that such people *suppose they will be heard for their many words.* The word Jesus uses (polulogia) means the great volume of their words, even if they are mere thoughtless babbling.

Jesus saw a real danger in all of this. He uses an imperative (command) in verse 8 to tell them they should not be like the heathen. Instead of letting the bad example of others mislead you, you ought to be warned by their example.

It does no good for the heathen to call upon God for anything, no matter how many words they might use. God does not hear the heathen because of their many words but because of their repentant heart. Only when the non-Christian calls upon God for salvation, believing that Christ died on the cross as a sacrifice for his sin and rose from the grave, will God hear and answer his prayer. The heathen pray to gods that have ears but do not hear. The Christian prays to a God who, time and time again, has proven His faithfulness to His people.

Then Jesus brings up another important consideration. He says that God knows our needs even before we ask. In other words, it is not as though we must inform God of every detail not to leave Him ignorant. On the contrary, to do this is to debase God and thus insult Him. So why should we forget His Omniscience in prayer?

The opposite error is also possible. Some may say that since God knows all our needs and is ever ready to help us, prayer is unnecessary, except for our benefit, relieving our hearts and making us more comfortable. Prayer is not just autosuggestion with psychological effects. *You have not, because you ask not or because you ask amiss* (James 4:2). Not to pray and ask is to reject God's commands and promises and to throw away how God Himself has appointed for us to secure His blessings.

Conclusion:

You may now ask yourself if you are a hypocrite or a heathen. Maybe you have been praying incorrectly, and God has just brought it to your attention. Perhaps you have been a hypocrite in some other area of your spiritual life. Being a hypocrite means you are wearing a mask and want people to see that mask. You are not on the inside what you appear to be on the outside. Will you remove the mask today?

Maybe you are not saved yet, and you know it. Stop being a heathen today. Give yourself to God and believe in Christ. God will hear that prayer and give you eternal life when you ask.

Review and Resolve:

1. Where are prayers more formalized in our culture?
2. What do you think about a set time for prayer, as did the Jews?
3. What kinds of repetition do we use in our Christian prayers today?
4. How do secret prayers help avoid 7 faults practiced by the Jews?
5. What is one prayer a heathen can pray that God will surely hear?
6. What is a good and practical interpretation of James 4:2?
7. Why might a person decide not to pray at all?
8. What is most encouraging to you in this lesson?

Chapter 22

The True Pattern for Prayer (Part II)

Pray then, in this way: 'Our Father who is in heaven, Hallowed by Your name. Your Kingdom come. Your will be done, on earth as it is in heaven. Give us this day our daily bread. And forgive us our debts, as we also have forgiven our debtors. And do not lead us into temptation, but deliver us from evil. For Yours is the kingdom, and the power, and the glory, forever. Amen.' For if you forgive men for their transgressions, your heavenly Father will also forgive you. But if you do not forgive men. Then your Father will not forgive your transgressions (Matthew 6:9-15).

This prayer has often been called "The Lord's Prayer." However, I consider John 17 the actual "Lord's Prayer." Matthew 6:9-13 is a model prayer given by Jesus to teach his disciples the proper format. It was, furthermore, not the purpose of Christ to have this prayer used in a liturgical way. There is no evidence that Jesus designed this prayer as a set formula. We should point out that there is no actual harm in a liturgical formula if one likes it, but no one should stick to just one formula for prayer. We should also point out there is good, not harm, in children learning this noble prayer.

We find this prayer also recorded in Luke 11:2-4 as a specimen or model of prayer in general. However, the Luke passage is later and at the request of one of His disciples. In contrast, the Matthew passage was at His initiation. In other words, the prayer was repeated twice by Jesus. That is not out of character with Jesus since He repeated many striking or important sayings at other times and in different connections. He offers the prayer in the two passages in varying terms. The Luke passage is the same prayer but in a briefer form.

Both Matthew and Luke are clear that Jesus taught this prayer to His disciples (Matthew 5:1; Luke 11:1). One of the first things that we should remember is that only a disciple of Christ may pray this prayer. I would rather not call this a child's or family prayer, not even "The Lord's Prayer." It is a disciple's prayer. By that, I mean only one wholly committed to God, His plan, and His kingdom can pray this prayer. This prayer only has meaning on the lips of a true disciple of Christ.

The prayer divides nicely into three sections. First, here is the invocation, which is the address to God. Then, there are the petitions related to God's interests, and finally, we have the petitions about our interests. These sections form our outline for the passage.

The Positive Admonitions (Matthew 5:9-15).

> **The Invocation.** Jesus tells us that we should address the Father when we pray. "Our Father" settles our relationship with God once and for all. Here a new connection in prayer is established. It does not mean He is any less God. It does not mean He has lost His might, majesty, and power. It simply means that His might, majesty, and power have become approachable to us.

An old Roman story tells how the Roman Emperor was enjoying his triumph. He had the privilege, which Rome gave to her great victors, of marching his troops through the streets of Rome with all his captured trophies and his prisoners in his train. So the Emperor was on the march with his forces. Cheering people lined the streets. The tall legionaries lined the street's edges to keep the people in their places. At one point on the triumphal route, there was a little platform where the Empress and her family sat to watch the Emperor go by in all the pride of his triumph. The Emperor's youngest son was on the platform with his mother. As the Emperor came near, the little boy jumped off the platform, burrowed through the crowd, and tried to dodge between the legs of the legionary and run onto the road to meet his father's chariot. The legionary stooped down and stopped him. He swung him up in his arms: "You can't do that, boy," he said. "Don't you know who that is in the chariot? That's the Emperor. You can't run out to his chariot." And the little lad laughed. "He may be your Emperor," he said, "but he's my father." That is precisely how the Christian feels toward God. The might, majesty, and power are the possessions of our Father.

Sometimes people pray to the Holy Spirit, and children often pray to Jesus. That is not wrong, but this text seems to indicate that our priority address in prayer is to the Father, the first person of the Godhead. When your children can understand, it is important that you teach them to pray to the Father. Teach them all the implications of the Father-child relationship we have with God.

The second thing we must recognize in this invocation is that God is in Heaven. The New Testament speaks of at least three heavens. (1) "The birds of the heaven" speaks of the atmosphere encircling the earth. (2) "Wonders in the heavens" speaks of the stellar spaces in which we see all these wonders of the stars and planets. (3) "Caught up even to the third heaven" (II Corinthians 12:2) refers to a place beyond the stellar spaces. It refers to the dwelling place of God, the place of the supreme manifestation of the presence of God––this place we cannot see, even with our modern telescopes.

The Petitions Seeking God's Interests (Matthew 6:9b-10). Jesus instructs us to seek the interests of God before we pursue our interests. He said: *Seek first the kingdom of God, and all these things will be added to you.* We must remember He is instructing us first to be concerned about God's interests. What are these interests?

His Name – May it be Hallowed. *Hallowed be Thy Name.* It means "Let your name be held holy." It means we are to regard it as different and give it a unique and special place. Anything or anyone who is "HOLY" (hagiadzo) is considered unique, exceptional, and separated from any other thing or person. Therefore, we are to treat God's name differently from all others and give it an absolutely unique position.

His name does not refer to just the name we call Him. It refers to his nature, character, or personality as revealed to us. That becomes clear when we see how the Bible writers use the expression "the name." The Psalmist said, *They that know Your name will trust in You* (Psalm 9:10). That does not mean those who know God is called YAHWEH will trust in Him. It means those who know what God is like, those who know God's nature and character, will put their trust in Him. Again, Psalm 20:7 says: *Some trust in chariots and some in horses, but we will remember the name of YAHWEH our God.* That does not mean the Psalmist will remember God is called YAHWEH in a difficult time. It means that at such a time, some will put their trust in human and material aids and defenses, but the Psalmist will remember God's nature and character; he will remember what God is like, and that memory will give him confidence.

Therefore, when we pray, *Hallowed be Your name.* It means, "Enable us to give to God the unique place which His nature and character deserve and demand." This prayer enables us to give God the unique place His nature demands.

His Kingdom –May it be Extended. We are to pray that God's kingdom will come. The technical reference here is to that Messianic reign that all devout Jews were expecting and which John and Jesus had been proclaiming as now near at hand.

His Will – May it be done. In this petition, God's children put their wills into complete harmony with their Father's will and thus into opposition to the will of His foes. We must recognize this submission when we pray this prayer. We must realize our lives are placed wholly under our Father's will, and we accept what His will, sends to us, which can include crosses, trials, sufferings, etc.

Your will be done on earth as it is in heaven. These words are devastating. Do we realize what we asking when we say those words? We are asking God to allow the conditions on earth to be the same as they are in heaven. Everything is under His control, and no human would get the chance to exercise his own will outside of God's will. That is how it will be during the Messianic reign of Jesus Christ. We call it the thousand-year reign of Christ. There may be a correlation between these two statements or petitions. Jesus spoke of the kingdom existing in the past (Abraham, Isaac, and Jacob, Luke 13:28); Matthew 8:11). He talked of it in the present (The Kingdom is in the disciples, (Luke 17:21). Of course, He is here speaking of the future Kingdom. This parallelism is often used in Hebrew literature and especially in the Psalms – *God is our refuge and strength, a very present help in trouble* (Psalm 46:1). Psalm 46:1 is an excellent example of parallelism––refuge and strength on one side and trouble on the other.

The second petition explains, amplifies, and defines the first. Finally, we have the perfect definition of the Kingdom of God in the broader sense. The kingdom of God is a society on earth where God's will is as perfectly done as in heaven. Here we have an explanation of how the Kingdom can be past, present, and future simultaneously. Any man who at any time in history perfectly did God's will is within the Kingdom. Still, since the world is very far from being a place where we universally do God's will is perfectly, the consummation of the Kingdom is still in the future. It is still something for which we must pray.

To be in the Kingdom is to obey the will of God. Immediately we see that the kingdom does not primarily have to do with nations, people, and countries. It is something that has to do with each one of us. The Kingdom is, in fact, the most personal thing in the world. The Kingdom demands the submission of my will, heart, and life. Only when each of us makes the personal decision and submission does the Kingdom come. To pray for the Kingdom of Heaven is to pray that we may submit our wills entirely to the will of God. Perhaps we should be careful what we pray for. If there is any portion of this sermon on the Mt. that you find yourself disagreeing with and you do not want to submit your will to the will of God, you cannot pray this prayer. The Kingdom, as spoken of in this passage, becomes a very personal thing and involves the utmost submission to the will of God.

The Petitions Seeking Man's Interest (Matthew 6:11-13).

For Daily Bread. One would think that this is the simplest petition of them all. But many interpreters have offered many interpretations of it. (1) The bread has been identified with the bread of the Lord's Supper. (2) It has been identified with the spiritual food of the Word of God. (3) It has been taken to stand for Jesus Himself since He called Himself *the bread of life* (John 6:33-35). (4) This petition has been taken in a purely Jewish sense and therefore taken to refer to the Heavenly Kingdom that the Jews expected to come. The difficulty is solved by understanding *daily* (epiousios). The Scriptures only use this word once. Origen, one of the early church fathers, held that Matthew had invented the word. But in recent years, a papyrus fragment turned up with the word on it. The fragment was a woman's shopping list referring to buying certain food for the coming day. The petition means God should give us our physical needs for the coming day. It is a simple prayer that God will supply us with our daily needs.

For Spiritual Renewal. It is essential to realize we must ask God to forgive us. This petition is the most frightening of all the requests in the Lord's Prayer. *Forgive us our debts as we forgive our debtors.* The literal meaning is: "Forgive us our sins in proportion as we forgive those who have sinned against us." Matthew goes on in verses 14 and 15 to clarify by showing us Jesus says in as plain a language as possible, *if we forgive others, God will forgive us.* But, if we refuse to forgive others, God will refuse to forgive us. For the believer, this is not a work of salvation but a product of salvation. Verse 12 deals not with salvation but with the relationship of the Child of God with his Father.

Therefore, it is quite clear that if we pray this petition with an unhealed breach, an unsettled quarrel in our lives, we are asking God not to forgive us. If we say, "I will never forgive or forget so-and-so for what he or she has done to me," we deliberately ask God not to forgive us. Human forgiveness and divine forgiveness are inextricably inter-combined. We cannot separate our not forgiving others from God not forgiving us––they are interlinked and interdependent. If we remember what we are doing when we take this petition on our lips, times will come when we would not dare to pray it.

For Guidance and Deliverance from Evil. *Lead* bothers many people. It seems to present God as an active agent in subjecting us to temptations––a thing specifically denied in James 1:13. The word *temptation* originally means *trial* or *test.* James 1:2 says God test or sift us, though He does not tempt us to do evil. No one understood temptation as well as Jesus, for the devil tempted him by every avenue of approach to all kinds of sin, but without success.

Review and Resolve:

1. What are the three sections this prayer divides into?
2. What is the significance of praying to *Our Father?*
3. Why would Jesus want us to Hallow God's name?
4. What is scary about praying that God's *will be done on earth as it is in heaven?*
5. What are two of the four different views on bread?
6. How do you feel about the discussion on forgiveness in this lesson?

Chapter 23

The Practice of Fasting

And whenever you fast, do not put on a gloomy face as the hypocrites do, for they neglect their appearance in order to be seen fasting by men. Truly I say to you, they have their reward in full. But you, when you fast, anoint your head, and wash your face so that you may not be seen fasting by men, but by your Father who is in secret; and your Father who sees in secret will repay you. (Matthew 6L16-18)

The third example Jesus gives of ostentatious piety is fasting. Remember, Jesus, is attempting to show the Jews, and His followers that they must do the right things for the right reasons. In the process, He picked three practices that were very close to the heart of every Jew, especially the Pharisees, and showed how they did the right things for the wrong reasons. He then explains to His disciples their attitude when they do the same things.

He did not demean almsgiving and prayer. So likewise, He does not speak against fasting. He assumes His disciples will fast. On the other hand, in another context, he defends His disciples for not fasting (Matthew 9:14-17). In the Sermon on the Mount, He is interested in condemning the abuses of the practice and exposing its dangers.

Fasting and the Old Testament:

The word means "to cover the mouth." It is not found in the Pentateuch but often occurs in the historical books and prophets. The expression used in the law is "afflicting the soul" (Leviticus 16:29-31; 23:27; Numbers 30:13), implying the sacrifice of the personal will, which gives fasting its value.

The Jews observed fasts with various degrees and strictness. When it was to last only a day, they abstained from food of every kind from evening to evening. In private fasts of a more prolonged character, it was merely the ordinary food from which they abstained. When they desired great humility of soul in repentance, it was not unusual to put on sackcloth, rend the garments, and scatter ashes over the head (II Samuel 13:19; I Kings 21:27).

I Samuel 7:6 says of Israel: ... *they drew water, and poured it out before the Lord, and fasted on that day.* To *Pour out your heart like water* (Lamentations 2:19) seems to denote inward dissolution through pain and misery. In connection with the fast, it would be a practical confession of misery and an act of deepest humiliation before the Lord.

The Mosaic law prescribed only one public occasion of strict fasting once a year on the great day of Atonement (Leviticus 16:29-31). Nevertheless, this observance seems always to have retained some prominence as *the fast* (Acts 27:9).

Also, the Hebrews, in earlier historical times, habitually fasted whenever they were in:

> Challenging, trying circumstances (I Samuel 1:7).
> Misfortune, bereavement (I Samuel 20:34; 31:13; II Samuel 1:12).
> Threatened judgments of God (II Samuel 12:16; I Kings 21:27).

Occasions of falling into grievous sin (Ezra 10:6).
Situations to avert heavy calamity (Esther 4:1).

Extraordinary fasts were appointed by the theocratic authorities on occasions of great national calamity so that the people might humble themselves before the Lord on account of their sins, thus avert His wrath, and get Him to look upon them again with His favor (Judges 20:26; I Samuel 7:6; II Chronicles 20:3; Joel 1:14; 2:12; Jeremiah 36:9; Ezra 8:21; Nehemiah 1:4). Other fasts were as follows:

> The 7th of the 4th month, Tammuz, July–the capture of Jerusalem (Jeremiah 52:6, 7; Zechariah 8:19).
> The 9th of the 5th month, Ab, August–the burning of the temple (II Kings 25:8; Zechariah 7:3; 8:19).
> The 3rd of the 7th month, Tishri, October–Death of Gedaliah (Zechariah 7:5; 8:19).
> The 10th of the 10th month, Tebeth, January–the commencement of the attack on Jerusalem (Zechariah 8:19; II Kings 25:1-4; Jeremiah 52:4).
> The fast of Esther was kept on the 13th of Adar (Esther 4:16).

With the growth of the Pharisaic spirit, the fasts became much more frequent generally until they assumed the form of ordinary pious exercise, so the Pharisees fasted regularly on the second and fifth day of every week (Matthew 9:14; Luke 18:12). Other Jewish sects, such as the Essenes, made their whole worship to consist principally of fasting.

Fasting and the New Testament:

The New Testament only references Jewish fasts in the mention of *the fasts* in Acts 27:9 (generally denoted the Day of Atonement) and the allusions to the weekly fasts (Matthew 9:14; Mark 2:18; Luke 5:33). These latter fasts originated sometime after the captivity (captivity of Israel by the Babylonians in

740 B.C. and the Assyrians in 721 B.C.) and were observed on the second and fifth days of the week, which were appointed as the days for public fasts (because Moses was supposed to have ascended the Mount for the second tablets of the law on a Thursday and to have returned on a Monday) seems to have been the reason selected for these private voluntary fasts.

Our Lord sternly rebuked the Pharisees for their hypocritical pretenses in the fasts, which they observed in our passages in Matthew 6:16-18. Furthermore, He abstained from appointing any fast as part of His religion. Matthew 17:21 and Mark 9:29 mention prayer and fasting to promote faith and as good works. Mention is also made of fasting in the Apostolic Church (Acts 13:3; 14:23; II Corinthians 6:5). In the last passage, the apostle probably refers to voluntary fasting as in II Corinthians 11:27. There, he makes a distinction between fasting and **"hunger and thirst."**

The Negative Admonition of Jesus:

What began as spiritual self-discipline, the Pharisees prostituted into an occasion for pompous self-righteousness. Some Jews who fasted would wear glum and pained expressions on their faces. They would go about their business unwashed and unkept to show they were fasting. Often, they would sprinkle ashes on their head and consequently became very dirty. People would not want to be around them. They did all to inform their peers they were fasting that day. What was once a sign of humiliation becoming a sign of self-righteous self-display.

Whatever the reasons, Jesus took it for granted that fasting would have a place in our Christian lives. His concern was, as with our giving and praying, we should not, like the hypocrites, draw attention to ourselves. As we have noted, their practice was to look dismal and to disfigure their faces. The word translated "disfigure" (KJV) or "Neglect their appearance" (NASV) means to "make to disappear" and so to "render invisible or unrecognizable." They may have neglected personal hygiene, covered their heads with sackcloth, or smeared their faces with ashes to look pale, wan, melancholy, and so outstandingly holy. All so their fasting might be seen and known by everybody. Again, Jesus calls them hypocrites.

The Positive Admonition of Jesus:

The first thing Jesus tells His disciples is to "anoint your hair." He probably means they should comb their hair to make themselves presentable. Possibly, it means putting ointment on their heads to make them smell good.

The second thing He says is to "wash your face." Again, do not walk around dirty and unkempt. He was not recommending anything unusual as if they were not to affect a particular sort of gaiety, righteousness, or holiness. He does not withdraw us from hypocrisy to lead us into another. He assumed they would wash and brush up daily, and fasting days were no different. Nobody was to suspect they were fasting. Everything should be as usual.

Again, He tells them they should practice this in secret. The purpose of fasting is not to advertise ourselves but to discipline ourselves. We are not to gain a reputation for ourselves but to express our humility before God and our concern for others in need. After all, this is between you and God and not between you and other men. Fulfilling these purposes will be reward enough. There are several good reasons for fasting within the context of modern-day Christianity. While not all Christians practice this discipline, and Scripture does not command it, others do because it is good for:

1. one's health to fast occasionally.
2. practicing self-discipline in one's life.
3. keeping us from becoming slaves to a particular habit.
4. giving us the ability to do without certain things.
5. causing us to appreciate certain things.
6. building a closer relationship with God.

Two Kinds of Piety:

Looking back over these verses, it is evident that Jesus has been contrasting two alternative kinds of piety, Pharisaic and Christian. These two are easily explained and distinguished. Pharisaic piety is ostentatious, motivated by vanity, and rewarded by men. Christian piety is secret, motivated by humility, and rewarded by God.

It may be helpful to look at the cause and effect of both forms to grasp the alternative even more clearly––first, the effect. Hypocritical religion is perverse because it is destructive. For example, we have seen that praying, giving, and fasting are all authentic activities in their own right. To pray is to seek God, to give is to serve others, and to fast is to discipline oneself. But the effect of hypocrisy is to destroy the integrity of these practices by turning each of them into an occasion for self-display.

What, then, is the cause? If we can isolate this, we can also find the remedy. Although one of the refrains of this passage is *...before men in order to be seen and praised by men,* it is not men with whom the hypocrite is obsessed, but himself. Our only reason for pleasing the men around us is that we may please ourselves. The remedy, then, is obvious. We must become so conscious of God that we cease to be self-conscious. And it is on this that Jesus concentrates.

Let me put it this way: absolute secrecy is impossible for any of us. It is not possible to do, say, or think anything in the absence of spectators. Even if no human being is there, God is watching us, not as a celestial policeman "snooping" to catch us doing something wrong, but as our loving heavenly Father, who is always looking for opportunities to bless us. So, the question is: which spectator matters to us more, earthly or heavenly, men or God?

The hypocrite performs his rituals *to be seen by men.* As we have already said, he is acting in a theater. His religion is a spectacle. The actual Christian is also aware of being watched, but the audience is God for him. Does the difference in audience cause a difference in performance? Yes! We can bluff a human audience; our performance can take them in. We can fool them into supposing we are genuine in giving, praying, and fasting when only acting. But God is not mocked; we cannot deceive Him. For God looks on the heart. That is why to do anything to be seen by men is bound to degrade it, while to do it to be seen by God is equally bound to dignify it.

Conclusion:

So, we must choose our audience carefully. If we prefer human spectators, we shall lose our Christian integrity. The same will happen if we become our audience. It is a bad situation if we become spectators of our prayer performance. We may lay on a lovely show for ourselves even in the privacy of our room. So, we must choose God as our audience as we secretly give, pray, and fast. God is there in the secret place with us. He hates hypocrisy and loves reality and truth. Our giving, praying, and fasting are authentic only when we are aware of His presence.

Review and Resolve:

1. Complete this sentence: Jesus is trying to teach the Jews and His followers that they must always do the _____ _____ for the _____ _____!
2. What interested you most about fasting in the Old Testament?
3. What kind of national calamity could be a reason for Christians to fast today?
4. Why did Jesus rebuke the Jews (Pharisees) of the New Testament?
5. Give three good reasons for fasting in our generation.
6. What positive guidelines does Jesus give us for fasting?
7. What is the difference between Pharisaic and Christian piety?
8. How can our audience determine our performance?

Chapter 24

Distorted Vision

Do not lay up for yourselves treasures upon earth, where moth and rust destroy, and where thieves break in and steal. But lay up for yourselves treasures in heaven, where neither moth nor rust destroys, and where thieves do not break in or steal; for where your treasure is, there will your heart be also. The lamp of the body is the eye; if therefore your eye is clear, your whole body will be full of light. But if your eye is bad, your whole body will be full of darkness. If therefore the light that is in you is darkness, how great is the darkness! No one can serve two masters; for either he will hate the one and love the other, or he will hold to one and despise the other. You cannot serve God and mammon. (Matthew 6:19-24)

Since childhood, we have heard that money talks. Listen to this dollar speak: "You hold me in your hand and call me yours. Yet may I not as well call you mine. See how easily I rule you? To gain me, you would all but die. I am invaluable as rain, essential as water. Without me, men and institutions would die. Yet I do not hold the power of life for them; I am futile without the stamp of your desire. I go nowhere unless you send or take me. I keep strange company. For me, men mock, love, and scorn character. Yet, I am appointed to the service of saints to give education to the growing mind and food to the starving bodies of the poor. My power is terrific. Handle me carefully and wisely, lest you become my servant rather than I yours." (Quote from Brian Dill, April 20, 2008)

Perhaps there are times when we forget the power money can have over us. Sometimes we get our thinking all mixed up on this subject. Will Rogers may have stated the issue well when he said, "Too many people spend money they haven't earned to buy things they don't want, to impress people they don't like."

Our world tends to emphasize the immediate. It is difficult to wait for anything, and temporal things have become so important to us. It seems the advertising world often rules our desires.

In contrast, however, we find it to be simple wisdom to acquire to oneself only those things which will last for a long time. Whether buying a suit of clothes, a car, a new carpet, or a piece of furniture, it is common sense to avoid shoddy goods and purchase things with solidity, permanence, and craftsmanship in them. Jesus is saying precisely that in this passage. He tells us to concentrate on something that will last, not on temporal things. He is speaking of things that have eternal implications.

Devotion is Determined by Treasure (Matthew 6:19-20).

It becomes clear, even common sense that our treasure will determine the kind of life we live. What we are devoted to is determined by the amount of treasure involved or how much of either we may have at any given time. Here are some of the things Jesus is teaching in this passage:

1. **Lasting Treasures are those Laid up in Heaven** (6:19-20). He speaks of the comparative durability of two treasures. It ought to be easy to decide which to collect. He implies because treasure on earth is corruptible, it is therefore insecure. In contrast, treasure in heaven is incorruptible and, consequently, secure.

It will help us face the question: "What was Jesus prohibiting when he told us not to lay up treasure for ourselves on earth?" However, it may help us if we understand what He is *not* forbidding. [1] There is no ban on possessions in themselves. Scripture nowhere forbids private property. [2] "Saving for a rainy day" is not forbidden to Christians. On the contrary, Scripture praises the ant for storing in the summer the food it will need in the winter and declares that the believer who makes no provision for his family is worse than an unbeliever (Proverbs 6:6ff; I Timothy 5:8). [3] We are not to despise but rather enjoy the good things our Creator has given us richly to enjoy.

What is Jesus referring to when He says, *Do not lay for yourselves treasures upon earth?* Perhaps He speaks of extravagant and luxurious living; the hardheartedness to the colossal need of the world's underprivileged people; the foolish fantasy that a person's life consists in the abundance of his possessions; and the materialism binding our hearts to the earth.

The result of this kind of treasure is that it is corruptible, *where moth and rust destroy, and where thieves break in and steal.* The Greek word for "rust" means "eating" and could refer to the corrosion caused by rusting, but equally to any devouring pest or insect. Nothing was safe in the ancient world. Nowadays, for us moderns, who try to protect our treasure with insecticides, rat poison, mouse traps, rustproof paints, and burglar alarms, our treasure disintegrates instead through inflation or devaluation, or an economic slump. Even if some of it lasts through this life, we can take none of it with us to the next. Job was right when he said, *Naked I came from my mother's womb, and naked I shall return* (Job 1:21).

While Jesus does not explain the treasure in heaven, He says it is incorruptible. To lay up treasure in heaven is to do anything on earth that lasts for eternity. Jesus was not teaching a doctrine of merit, as if we could accumulate a kind of credit account in heaven by good deeds done on earth. The Gospel denies that, and He spoke to disciples who already had eternal life. So, Jesus is not teaching a kind of salvation by works here.

Probably, what Jesus refers to are things like a Christlike character, the increase of faith, hope, and love, all of which Paul said, "abide" (I Corinthians 13:13). He may also be speaking about growth in the knowledge of Christ, the active endeavor to introduce others to Christ, and the use of our money for causes which spread the gospel of Christ. All these are temporal activities with eternal consequences. Furthermore, treasure in heaven is secure because it cannot corrupt as treasure on earth. Jesus seems to say, "If it's a safe investment you are after, nothing could be safer than this."

2. **Their Location Determines One's Affection** (6:21). The Sermon on the Mount repeatedly refers to the "heart." One of the reasons is that this sermon has to do with heart religion as opposed to outward religion. Constantly, Jesus has thrust His application of the truth by telling us that this is the way we should function inside rather than outside. Unsurprisingly, He does the same thing with the issue of money and how we use it.

In verse 21, Jesus declares that our heart always follows our treasure, whether down to earth or up to heaven. If everything a man values and sets his heart upon is on earth, then all his interests will be upon the earth. He will have no interest in any world beyond this world. If, throughout his life, a man sets his eyes on eternity, he will evaluate the things of this world lightly. Further, suppose everything a man counts as valuable is on earth. In that case, he will leave earth reluctantly and grudgingly, but if his thoughts have ever been in the world beyond, he will leave this world with gladness because he finally goes to God.

Distorted Vision may be the Result (Matthew 6:22-23).

Jesus gives us an illustration of the result of an improper concern for possessions in this world. It has to do with our spiritual vision.

William Barclay writes about these verses: "The idea behind this passage is one of childlike simplicity. The eye is regarded as the window by which the light gets into the whole body. The color and state of the window decide what light gets into a room. If the window is clear, clean, and undistorted, the light will come flooding into the room, and will illuminate every corner of it. If the glass of the window is colored or frosted, distorted, dirty, or obscure, the light will be hindered, and the room will not be lit up ... So then, says Jesus, the light which gets into any man's heart and soul and being depends on the spiritual state of the eye through which it has to pass, for the eye is the window of the whole body."

Let me ask you a question. Do you see spiritual things clearly? Or is your vision of God and His will for your life clouded by spiritual cataracts or near-sightedness brought on by an unhealthy preoccupation with things? I am convinced this is true for many Christians, particularly those living amid western affluence. Now and then, people like this complain to me that they cannot understand the Bible or God that seems far away from them. Sometimes they are confused about the Christian life or God's will for them.

Well, it is not surprising. And, what is more, it always will be this way for one who knows his way around a supermarket or a brokerage house more than he knows his way around the New Testament.

Although Jesus did not direct us away from possessions themselves, He did warn us against losing our spiritual vision because of them. There is yet another consideration in these verses. The word the KJV translates as *single,* the NASV translates as *clear,* and the translators of the RSV and Phillips translate *sound,* as the Greek word haplous. In some texts, the word means *simple* or *simplicity.* In other texts, it means *generosity.* The translators of the New Scofield Bible recognized this truth when they came to Romans 20:8, for in that verse, the word *simplicity* (KJV) is changed to *liberality* so that the text now reads: *He that giveth let him do it with liberality.* In James 1:5, we read, *If any of you lack wisdom, let him ask of God, who giveth to all men liberally.* The word occurs in this same sense at least three times in II Corinthians 8:2; 9:11, 13, and once in Colossians 3:22.

I believe this sense of the word is present here in Christ's teaching. The *single eye* is the *generous eye.* And if that is the case, then Jesus is promoting a generous spirit regarding our money. How can you tell whether riches have clouded your spiritual vision? You may determine the answer by how generous you are with the goods God has given to you.

Double Allegiance is Impossible (Matthew 6:24).

Finally, we come to verse 24, a principle many people today cannot live with. The verse deals with the mutually exclusive nature of serving God and riches at the same time. Jesus could not have said this more clearly or more obviously. It should be a heart-searching question for all Christians. Ask yourself this: "Can anything be more insulting to God, who has redeemed us from the slavery of sin, put us in Christ, and given us all things richly to enjoy than to take the name of our God upon us, to be called by His name, and then to demonstrate by every action and every decision of life that we actually serve money or some other passion?"

In discussing this verse, Dr. D. Martyn Lloyd-Jones tells the story of a farmer who one day reported to his wife with great joy that his best cow had given birth to twin calves, one red, and one white. He said, "The Lord has led me to dedicate one of the calves to Him. First, we will raise them together, and then when the time comes to sell them, we will keep the proceeds from one calf and give the proceeds from the other to the Lord's work."

His wife asked which calf he would dedicate to the Lord, but he answered there was yet time to decide. "We will treat them both in the same way," he said, "and when the time comes, we will sell them as I have said."

Several months later, the man entered the kitchen looking sad and miserable. When his wife asked what troubled him, he said, "I have bad news for you. The Lord's calf died."

"But," said his wife, "You had not yet decided which was the Lord's calf."

"Oh yes," he said. "I had always determined that it was to be the white one, and it is the white one that is dead."

The Lord's calf always dies unless we are clear about our service to Him and the true nature of our possessions. Who owns your possessions? The Lord Jesus Christ tells us that either God owns them, and you serve Him, or else your possessions own you, and you serve them. In any case, no one ever really possesses them himself, although many people think they do. May God give us each the victory that comes when we turn over our gifts, wealth, time, friends, ambitions, and talents to Him, and we use them to establish indestructible riches in heaven.

Review and Resolve:

1. What do you think is the world's attitude about money and how does that affect us as Christians?
2. What are the three things that Jesus is *not* forbidding in this passage?
3. What is the difference in this passage between that which is corruptible and that which is incorruptible?
4. What does Jesus mean in verse 21: *...for where your treasure is, there will your heart be also?*
5. How clear are you on what part of your wealth belongs to God? Which calf is God's?
6. Do you see some of the near-sightedness brought on by an unhealthy preoccupation with things in some people around you?

Chapter 25

Worry, And It's Cure

For this reason I say to you, do not be anxious for your life as to what you shall eat, or what you shall drink; nor for your body, as to what you shall put on. Is not life more than food, and the body than clothing? Look at the birds of the air, that they do not sow, neither do they reap, nor gather into barns, and yet your heavenly Father feeds them. Are you not worth much more than they? And which of you by being anxious can add a single cubit to his life's span? And why are you anxious about clothing? Observe how the lilies of the field grow; they do not toil nor do they spin. Yet I say to you that even Solomon in all his glory did not clothe himself like one of these. But if God so arrays the grass of the field, which is alive today and tomorrow is thrown into the furnace will He not much more do so for you, O men of little faith? Do not be anxious then, saying, 'What shall we eat?' or 'What shall we drink?' or 'With what shall we clothe ourselves?' For all these things the Gentiles eagerly seek; for your heavenly Father knows that you need all these things. But seek first His kingdom and His righteousness; and all these things shall be added to you. Therefore, do not be anxious for tomorrow; for tomorrow will care for itself. Each day has enough trouble of its own (Matthew 6:25-34).

If you look up the word "worry" in the dictionary, you will find this: "To be uneasy in the mind; feel anxiety about something; to fret."

Worry is something many people have great difficulty with. An actor visiting a psychiatrist for years says, "I must be the only guy who ever spent $10,000 on a couch and still doesn't own it.

Sometimes people worry about the strangest things. R. C. Trench, who many years ago was the Protestant Archbishop of Dublin, had a morbid fear of becoming paralyzed. One evening at a party, the lady he sat beside at dinner heard him muttering mournfully to himself, "It has finally happened. There is total insensibility in my right limb."

"Your Grace," said the lady, "It may comfort you to learn that it is my leg you are pinching."

In 1961, *Time Magazine* published a cover story on the presence of anxiety in America entitled *Guilt and Anxiety*. It stated that the breakdown of faith in God coupled with the accelerated pace and high tension of modern life had produced intense anxiety in millions of people, so much so that it could be correct to say worry is one of the most widespread and debilitating ailments of our time.

Time wrote, "Not merely the black statistics of murder, suicide, alcoholism, and divorce betray anxiety (or that form of guilt), but almost any innocent everyday act: the limp or over-hearty handshake, the second pack of cigarettes or the third martini, the forgotten appointment, the stammer in mid-sentence, the wasted hour before the TV set, the spanked child, the new car unpaid for." The writers added that these symptoms are intensified for many of us by the dominant American myths that "the old can grow young, the indecisive can become leaders of men, the housewives can become glamour girls, the glamour girls can become actresses" (March 31, 1961, pp. 44, 46).

In this analysis, *Time* was, I believe, at its best. I realize that 1961 was a long time ago. However, the more we encounter people, we recognize worry is all around us. That which *Time* spoke of in 1961 has only gotten worse today, for it is true that worry is with us, and millions of people (many Christians) are troubled by it. While it is not well defined, it is real, and we must deal with it. Perhaps we can learn from Jesus how to deal with worry.

Because of time, we must deal with the section on money and the section on anxiety separately. However, we do not want to miss the significance of the introductory words, *Therefore I tell you* (KJV) or *For this reason I say to you* (NASV). We must begin by relating this *Therefore* to the conclusion of Jesus in the previous context. He calls us to thought before He calls us to action. Only when we have grasped with our minds the comparative durability of the two treasures (corruptible and incorruptible), the relative usefulness of the two eye conditions (light and darkness), and the comparative worth of the two masters (God and mammon), are we ready to make our choice. Only when we have made our choice, for heavenly treasure, for light, for God, *Therefore, I tell you, This is how you must behave: do not be anxious about your life...nor about your body...but seek first His kingdom and His righteousness* (vs. 25, 33).

It will help to precisely know what Jesus forbids and what He demands. First, we find the words *do not be anxious* (NASV). The KJV has it, *take no thought for the morrow.* Wycliffe had it right: *Be not busy to your life.* Tyndale says, *Be not careful for your life.* They used the word "careful" in the literal sense of "full of care." The older versions were more accurate. It is not ordinary, prudent foresight, such as is becoming to a man, that Jesus forbids; it is worry. Jesus is not advocating a shiftless, thriftless, reckless, thoughtless, or improvident life attitude. He forbids a care-worn, worried fear that takes all the joy out of life.

Jesus is teaching a lesson His countrymen well knew. He is teaching of prudence, forethought, serenity, and trust all combined. In doing so, He gives us seven different arguments and defenses against worry.

1. **God Gave Us Life.** If He gave us life, surely, we can trust Him for the lesser things associated with life (6:25). Surely, we can trust Him to provide us with food to sustain life. If God gave us bodies, surely, we can trust Him for clothing to put on that body. When God provides us with a gift beyond price, we can be sure He will not be mean, stingy, careless, and forgetful about much less costly gifts. We can trust God to meet those needs. Jesus immediately brings us and our needs for life into a relationship with God, which is vital in this passage.

2. **God Cares for The Birds of The Air.** So, He will take care of you (6:26). If God takes care of the animals, will He not take care of the Redeemed? There is no worry in the lives of birds, no attempt to pile up goods for an unforeseen and unforeseeable future. Yet, their lives go on. More than one Jewish Rabbi was fascinated how the animals are cared for. Rabbi Simeon said, "In my life, I have never seen a stag as a dryer of figs, or a lion as a porter, or a fox as a merchant, yet they are all nourished without worry. If they, who are created to serve me, are nourished without worry, how much more ought I, who am created to serve my Maker, to be nourished without worry; but I have corrupted my ways, and so I have impaired my substance."

The point that Jesus is making is not that the birds do not work; I've heard it said that no one works harder than the average sparrow to make a living. The point here is that they do not worry. There is not to be found in them a man's straining to see a future that he cannot see, nor a man's seeking to find security in things stored up and accumulated against the future.

3. **Worry is a Useless Activity** (6:27). It is uncertain whether the last word of His question should translate as *span of life* or *stature*. We can trans-late it either way. Adding *one cubit* (18 inches) to our stature would be a remarkable feat, although God does it to all of us between our child-hood and adult life. To add a period of time to our lifespan is also out-side our competence. A human being cannot achieve this by himself.

Indeed, far from lengthening his life, worry may very well shorten it, as we all know. Often, I say to people, "Don't worry. It won't change anything anyway." There are certain things and circumstances which we cannot change and worrying about them is useless. It will not help.

4. **God Takes Care of The Field Flowers.** If God can take care of the flowers of the fields (created plants), He can take care of you (His Redeemed) (6:20-30). The lilies were the scarlet poppies and anemones. They bloomed one day on the hillsides of Palestine, yet in their brief life, God clothed them with a beauty surpassing the beauty of kings' robes. When the flowers died, they were burned.

The point is this. The Palestinians set their clay oven on bricks over the fire. Then, when they desired to raise the temperature quickly, they flung handfuls of dried grasses and wildflowers inside the oven. The flowers had but one day of life, and then they were set on fire to help a woman heat an oven when baking in a hurry. Yet God clothes them with a beauty beyond man's power to imitate. If God gives such beauty to a short-lived flower, how much more will He care for a human created in His image? Surely the generosity which is so lavish to the flower will not be forgetful of man, the crown of creation.

Listen to what Martin Luther's words about these birds and flowers: "He is making the birds our schoolmaster and teachers. It is a great and abiding disgrace to us that in the Gospel a helpless sparrow should become a theologian and a preacher to the wisest of men ... Whenever you listen to a nightingale, therefore, you are listening to an excellent preacher ... It is as if he were saying 'I prefer to be in the Lord's kitchen. He has made heaven and earth, and He Himself is the cook and the host. Every day He feeds and nourishes innumerable little birds out of his hand.'" And Charles Spurgeon said: "Lovely lilies, how you rebuke our foolish nervousness!"

Notice that Jesus does not say in verse 26 that the birds have a heavenly father, but rather that we have. If the Creator cares for His creatures, we may be even more sure that the Father will look after His children.

5. **Worry is Not Characteristic of God's Children.** Heathens do not know God personally or what God is like (6:32), therefore they worry. Worry is essentially distrust of God. Such a distrust may be understandable in a heathen who believes in a jealous, capricious, unpredictable god. Still, it is beyond comprehension in one who has learned to call God by the name "Father."

6. **Replace Your desires With God's Desires (6:33).** In this verse, Jesus gives us two ways in which to defeat worry:

- **The first is to seek or concentrate upon the kingdom of God.** He referred to this in 6:10 when He stated that we must want and pray for the kingdom to come on earth. The kingdom of God is God's will for us and concentrating on the doing and acceptance of God's will is the way to defeat worry. We know how great love can drive out every other concern. Such love can inspire a man's work, intensify his study, purify his life, and dominate his whole being. It was Jesus' conviction that worry is banished when God becomes the dominating power in our lives.

- **We must also concentrate on the righteousness of God.** There is a difference between God's kingdom and His righteousness. God's kingdom exists only where Jesus Christ is consciously acknowledged. To be in His kingdom is synonymous with enjoying His salvation. Only the born-again have seen and entered the kingdom. And to see it first is to spread the good news of salvation in Christ. But God's righteousness is a broader concept than God's kingdom. It includes that individual and social righteousness that applies to every person who has ever lived. The Hebrew prophets denounced injustice not only in Israel and Judah but also in the surrounding heathen nations.

God hates injustice and loves righteousness everywhere. God is both the Creator and the Judge of all men.

God wants us to make His righteousness attractive in our personal, family, business, national, and international life. Then people outside God's kingdom to whom it applies will desire it. To spread God's kingdom, we must evangelize others. To spread God's righteousness, we must also evangelize, but we shall also engage in social action and endeavor to spread throughout the community those higher standards and integrity of righteousness which are pleasing to God.

7. **We Defeat Worry One Day At a Time** (6:34).

The Jews had a saying: "Do not worry over tomorrow's evils, for you know not what today will bring forth. Perhaps tomorrow you will not be alive, and you will have worried for a world which will not be yours." If we live each day as it comes and do each task as it appears, then the sum of all the days is bound to be good. Therefore, it is Jesus' advice that we should handle the demands of each day as it comes, without worrying about the unknown future and the things which may never happen.

Conclusion:

Robert Frost once said: "The reason why worry kills more people than work is that more people worry than work." Worry is the advance interest you pay on troubles that seldom come. We must remember that the little birds of the field have God as their caterer.

We can get rid of worry by thinking about and concentrating on God, His Kingdom, and His righteousness. Do you know God? Do you strive for His righteousness? Do you want to see His kingdom come to pass and others come to know Christ as their Savior? Are you close to God, and do you trust

Him more than anything or anyone else? All of that will help you deal with worry in your life!

Review and Resolve:

1. What is the relationship between the discussion on money (6:19-24) and this discussion on worry (6:25-34)?
2. What are Jesus' seven arguments, and what do you think of each?

Chapter 26

No Man Can Judge Another

Do not judge lest you be judged. For in the way you judge, you will be judged; and by your standard of measure, it will be measured to you. And why do you look at the speck that is in your brother's eye, but do not notice the log that is in your own eye? Or how can you say to your brother, 'Let me take the speck out of your eye,' and behold, the log is in your own eye?' You hypocrite, first take the log out of your own eye, and then you will see clearly to take the speck out of your brother's eye (Matthew 7:1-5).

The voice over the phone said: "I sent my little son, James, to your store for five pounds of apples, and I find on weighing them that you sent only four and a quarter pounds." The Grocer said: "Madam, my scales are regularly inspected and are correct. Have you weighed little James?"

It impresses me how many of us are willing to make judgments without enough accurate information. There have been embarrassing illustrations of this in history. For instance: Here's how the *"Chicago Times"* in 1865 evaluated Lincoln's Gettysburg Address in commenting on it the day after its delivery: "The cheek of every American must tingle with shame as he reads the silly, flat, and dish-watery utterances of a man who has to be pointed out to intelligent foreigners as President of the United States."

Also, in many public speeches, the great Daniel Webster expressed his doubt concerning the ultimate success of the American railroad system. He argued that frost on the rails would prevent the train from moving, or, if it did move, they could not bring it to a stop.

And most of the people who loaned money to Robert Fulton to develop his proposed steamboat did so with the stipulation that their names be kept secret for fear others might ridicule them for backing such an absurd idea.

Listen to this one! A six-year-old lad came home with a note from his teacher who suggested he be taken out of school as he was "too stupid to learn." That boy was Thomas A. Edison. And I love this one! Benjamin Franklin's mother-in-law hesitated at letting her daughter marry a printer. After all, there were already two printing offices in the United States, and she feared the country might be unable to support a third.

This issue of criticism and judging one another is the issue that Jesus deals with as we enter Matthew 7. Next, He begins to deal with relationships, and we need this teaching in every culture, society, and generation.

Please note that Matthew 7 consists of several self-contained paragraphs. Their link to each other is not readily apparent, and this chapter does not follow the form of the previous chapter. As a result, some believe that Matthew 7 does not belong here, that Matthew did some "scissors and paste" work on the book, and that he did it a trifle clumsily. But there is a connecting thread that runs through this chapter, however loosely, and is the thread of relationships. Since describing a Christian's character, influence, righteousness, piety, and ambition, it seems logical that Jesus should finally concentrate on a person's relationships.

The relationship in the passage before us is that of our brother, in whose eye we may discern a splinter and whom we have a responsibility to help, not judge. So often, we ask ourselves, "How should a Christian behave towards a fellow member who has misbehaved?" Has Jesus any instructions about discipline within His community? Yes, in such a situation, He forbids two alternatives and then commends a third, a better and more "Christian way."

The Christian is NOT to be a Judge (Matthew 7:1-2).

Jesus' words *Do not judge lest you be judged* are well known but much misunderstood. We must first reject what He does not mean by these words. Based on this verse, we cannot accept Tolstoy's belief, that "Christ totally forbids the human institution of any law court" and that He "could mean nothing else by those words." Jesus cannot mean this because the context does not refer to judges in courts of law but rather to the responsibility of individuals to one another. Furthermore, other places in Scripture give judgment responsibility to rulers and civil authorities.

Jesus also cannot be understood to mean that we suspend our critical faculties with other people, turn a blind eye to their faults (pretending not to notice them), eschew all criticism, and refuse to discern between truth and error, goodness and evil. This ability is not possible for the following three reasons:

1. **Because it would be dishonest, hypocritical behavior.** From this and other passages, we know Christ's love of integrity and hatred of hypocrisy.

2. **Because it would contradict the nature of man.** God created man with the ability to make value judgments, and man must make such judgments to be satisfied.

3. **Much of Christ's teaching assumes we will (indeed should) use our critical powers.** This power is something found throughout the Word of God. He calls us to be different from the world and develop a righteousness exceeding that of the Pharisees. We must not be like

hypocrites in our piety or heathen in our ambition. To do that, we must first evaluate their performance and judge it. This necessity of using our critical powers is further shown in 7:6 to avoid giving *what is holy* to dogs or pearls to pigs. In 7:15 we are to be aware of false prophets.

4. What does Jesus mean when He says, *Do not judge lest you be judged?* The word Jesus uses for "Judgement" is the Greek word krima. It may be used for judgment by men and judgment by God. It is a word that has to do with not only the judgment of a person but also the result, condemnation, and sentence. In other words, we are not to be the ones to condemn and sentence others. The follower of Jesus is still a "critic" in the sense of using his powers of discernment but not a "judge" in the sense of being censorious. Censoriousness is a compound sin consisting of several unpleasant ingredients. It does not mean to assess people critically but to judge them harshly. This kind of person is a faultfinder who is negative and destructive towards others and enjoys actively seeking out their failings.

To be this kind of person is to set oneself up as a censor and claim the competence and authority to judge one's fellow men. Men are not our servants, responsible to us. We are neither their lord nor their judge. Paul spoke to this in Romans 14:4 when he said: *Who are you to pass judgment on the servant of another? It is before his own master that he stands or falls.* He applies the same truth to himself in I Corinthians 4:4-5.

The simple and vital point Paul makes in these verses is that man is not God. No human being is qualified to judge his fellow humans, for we cannot read each other's hearts or assess each other's motives. To be censorious is to presume arrogantly, anticipate the day of judgment, and usurp the divine judge's prerogative to be God.

Not only are we not the judge, but we are among the judged and shall be judged with greater strictness ourselves if we dare to judge others (v. 2). The rationale should be clear. If we pose as judges, we cannot plead ignorance of the law we claim to be able to administer. If we enjoy occupying the bench, we must not be surprised to find ourselves on the dock.

To sum up, the command not to judge is not a requirement to be blind but rather a plea to be generous. Jesus does not tell us to cease to be men (by suspending our critical powers, which help to distinguish us from animals) but to renounce the presumptuous ambitions to be God (by setting ourselves up as judges.)

The Christian is NOT to be a Hypocrite (Matthew 7:3-4).

Jesus now tells His famous little parable about foreign bodies in people's eyes, specks of dust on the one hand and logs or beam on the other. Earlier, Jesus exposed hypocrisy concerning God, namely practicing our piety before men to be seen by them; now, He exposes it in relation to others, namely meddling with their minor offenses, while failing to deal with our own more serious faults. Here is another reason we are unfit to be judges: not only because we are fallible humans (and not God), but also because we are fallen humans. The fall has made us all sinners. So, we are in no position to stand in judgment of our fellow sinners; we disqualified ourselves from the bench.

The picture shown in these verses is ludicrous to the extreme. It is that of someone struggling with the delicate operation of removing a speck of dirt from a friend's eye while a vast plank in his eye entirely obscures his vision. People have a fatal tendency to exaggerate the faults of others and minimize the gravity of their own. As a result, they find it impossible to be strictly objective and impartial. We seem to have a rosy view of ourselves and a judicial view of others. Jesus calls those who do such a thing "hypocrites" (v. 5).

Instead, we should apply to ourselves at least as strict and critical a standard as we use for others. The Apostle Paul said it this way: *If we judge ourselves truly, we should not be judged* (I Corinthians 11:31). We should not only escape the judgment of God; we would also be in a position humbly and gently to help an erring brother. Having first removed the log from our eye, we would see clearly to take the speck from his.

Rather be a Christian Brother (Matthew 7:5).

In verse 5, Jesus again separates His followers from the hypocrites. He counsels us to accomplish a good ministry of admonition. We are to first take the log out of our eye. *Then you will see clearly to take the speck out of your brother's eye.*

Some people believe that in this little parable (The Speck and the Log), Jesus tells us we must not act as moral ophthalmologists, meddle with other people's eyes, and tell us instead to mind our business. This interpretation is not valid! The fact that censoriousness and hypocrisy are forbidden does not relieve us of brotherly responsibility towards one another. On the contrary, Jesus was later to teach that if our brother sins against us, our first duty (though usually neglected) is *go and tell him his fault between you and him alone* (Matthew 18:15). The same obligation is laid upon us here. In certain circumstances, God forbids us to interfere when we have not removed an even bigger foreign body from our eyes. But in other cases, Jesus commands us to reprove and correct our brother. Once we have dealt with our eye trouble, we shall see clearly to deal with his. A bit of dirt in his eye is foreign and doesn't belong there. It is always alien, usually painful, and sometimes dangerous. To leave it there, and make no attempt to remove it, would hardly be consistent with brotherly love.

Conclusion:

It is evident that Jesus is not condemning criticism as such, but rather the criticism of others when we exercise no comparable self-criticism; nor correction, but rather the correction of others when we have not first corrected ourselves. However, once we have dealt with our eye trouble, it is our brotherly responsibility to help our brother with his own. The standard of Jesus for relationships in the Christian culture is high and healthy. In all our attitudes and behavior toward others, we are neither the judge (becoming harsh, censorious, and condemning) nor the hypocrite (blaming others while excusing ourselves). Still, the brother cares for others so much that we first blame and correct ourselves and then seek to be constructive in the help we give them.

Chrysostom (one of the early church fathers) alluded to someone who had sinned and said: "Correct him, but not as a foe, nor as an adversary exacting a penalty, but as a physician providing medicines!" Yes, even more, as a loving brother anxious to rescue and restore him.

We must be cautious in our judgment of other people. Longfellow once said: "If we could only read the secret history of our enemies, we would find in each man's life, sorrow and suffering enough to disarm all hostility." A Japanese proverb says: "Search seven times before you suspect anyone."

Indeed, we must consider ourselves before we judge anyone. And even then, we must lovingly regard our brothers, not as a judge who condemns them. Why? Because we are not God, and we do not have the right to do so!

Review and Resolve:

1. What is the connecting thread that runs throughout Matthew 7?
2. What are three good reasons why Jesus cannot mean we suspend our critical faculties concerning other people?
3. What is significant about the word "Judgment" (krima)?
4. What is the meaning of the illustration Jesus uses (The Speck and the Log)?
5. Why do you think Jesus constantly wants to contrast His followers with hypocrites?
6. Why must we self-evaluate before criticizing one of our brothers?

Chapter 27

Just For the Asking

Ask, and it shall be given to you; seek, and you shall find; knock, and it shall be opened to you. For everyone who asks receives, and he who seeks finds, and to him who knocks it shall be opened. Or what man is there among you, when his son shall ask him for a loaf, will give him a stone? Or if he shall ask for a fish, he will not give him a snake, will he? If you then, being evil, know how to give good gifts to your children, how much more shall you Father who is in heaven give what is good to those who ask him! Therefore, however, you want people to treat you, so treat them, for this is the Law and the Prophets (Matthew 7:7-12).

If you remember, the Lord Jesus has been giving us the practice of the kingdom beginning with chapter 6 of Matthew. He talks about the following and we have observed each one in some detail: The Practice of Almsgiving (6:1-4).

The Practice of Prayer (6:5-15).
The Practice of Fasting (6:16-18).
The Practice of Using Money (6:19-24).
The Practice of Worry (6:25-34).
The Practice of Judging (7:1-6).
And Now, The Practice of Asking (7:7-12).

In recent passages, Jesus has dealt with our relationships and practices with our fellow men. Now He turns to our relationship with our heavenly Father once again, which should not surprise us. It is fitting that this should follow on the heels of the previous passage, where we are given the Christian duty of discrimination (not judging others, not casting pearls before pigs, and being helpful without hypocritical). To do such a thing without divine guidance and grace is much too challenging.

What we want to do in this section is look at the promises Jesus makes in this passage and then observe some of the existing problems.

The Promises Jesus Makes:

As we have seen, this passage is not the first instruction Jesus gave on prayer in this sermon. He has warned us against acting like the Pharisees and against functioning as the pagans do in their formalism and repetition. Further, He gave us His model for prayer in what we call "The Lord's Prayer." In this passage, He gives us significant promises concerning our prayer life. These promises become a motivation for us to have a strong prayer life. Calvin said: "Nothing is better adapted to excite us to prayer than a full conviction that we shall be heard." Luther said, "Christ wants to lure us away from timidity, to remove our doubts, and to have us go ahead confidently and boldly." Therefore, the promises that Christ gives to us are critical. They form the value and the motivation for prayer in our lives. Let's look at these promises.

The Repetition:

Jesus uses the verbs "Ask, Seek, and Knock." He looks to imprint His promises on our minds and memories with the hammer blows of repetition. He may have deliberately placed these verbs in an ascending scale of urgency, and all three verbs are present imperatives from a grammatical point of view. In other words, they are all commands. Therefore, they indicate the persistence with which we should make our requests known to God. And perhaps more important than that, they are commands. These imperatives show continuous action; *Keep on asking, keep on seeking, keep on knocking.* Also, there are two words for "knock" in Greek, one which refers to an unceremonious pounding, the other to a polite knock. Jesus used the latter here. So, a timid, polite knock is meant?

It is also important to note that Jesus expresses these promises in universal statements: *For everyone who asks receives, and he who seeks finds, and to him who knocks it shall be opened (v. 8).* Obviously, He takes into consideration some presuppositions in making such universal statements. We will speak about some of that later in our lesson.

The Illustration which Jesus uses:

After giving the command and stating the universal principles, Jesus illustrates His promises through a parable (vs. 9-11). He uses an illustration with which all of his hearers would be familiar: a child coming to a father with a request. What father would give his son a stone in place of a loaf of bread and a snake instead of a fish? In other words, if the child asks for something wholesome to eat (bread and fish), will he receive rather something unwholesome, even inedible (a stone) and positively harmful (a poisonous snake)? Of course not.

Jesus assumes, even asserts, the inherent sinfulness of human nature. In other words, even though they are evil and selfish, parents still love their children and give them only good gifts. The force of this parable lies in contrast. It is the "how much more argument." Suppose human parents (although evil) know how to give good gifts to their children. How much more will our heavenly Father (who is not evil but totally and completely good) give good things to those who ask Him (v. 11)?

What would be more straightforward than this concept of prayer? If we belong to Christ, God is our Father, we are His children, and prayer is coming to Him with our requests. The trouble is that for many of us, it seems too simple, even simplistic. In all of our sophistication, we say we cannot believe it. In any case, it does not altogether tally with our experience. So, we turn from Christ's prayer promises to our prayer problems.

The Problems Men Raise:

Confronted by the straightforward promises of Jesus, *Ask, and it will be given you; seek, and you will find,* people tend to raise several objections which we need to consider.

Prayer is Unseemly:

Some say this encouragement to pray presents a false picture of God. It implies we must tell Him what we lack or bully Him into giving us what we need. After all, Jesus Himself said earlier that our heavenly Father knows all our needs and cares for us anyway. So, why should we think His gifts are dependent on our asking? Do human parents wait before supplying their children's needs until they ask for them? Why pray?

We do not find the answer in the idea that we must inform God of our needs because He is ignorant or reluctant, and we must persuade Him to meet our needs. The answer has to do with us, not with God. The question is not whether He is ready to give but whether we are prepared to receive. So, in prayer, we do not master God but ourselves to submit to God. Even when Jacob prevailed on God, what happened is that God triumphed over him, bringing him to the point of surrender when he was able to receive the blessing which God had all the time been longing to give him.

The truth is that the Father never spoils His children. He does not shower us with gifts whether we want them or not, whether we are ready for them. Instead, The Father waits until we recognize our need to turn to Him humbly. For this reason, He said, *Ask, and it will be given to you,"* and why

James added, *You do not have because you do not ask (James 4:2)*. Prayer then is theological and correct. It is the way God Himself has chosen for us to express our conscious need to Him and our humble dependence on Him.

Prayer is Unnecessary:

This problem arises more from experience than from theology. Some Christians look around themselves and observe that people are getting good things without prayer. They seem to receive without prayer the very stuff we receive with it. They get what they need by working for it, not praying for it. The farmer gets a good crop by labor; the mother gets her baby by medical skill; the family balances its budget by the wage-earning of the dad and perhaps others. Some feel tempted to say, "This proves that prayer doesn't make an ounce of difference; it's so much wasted breath."

How do we answer such an argument? First, let's be sure we understand the primary purpose of prayer is not only to get what we can. It is to build more deeply our relationship with our heavenly Father. If we pray only to "GET," we are praying for all the wrong reasons. The gifts God gives us as a result of prayer are a by-product of the great relationship. We must also distinguish between the gifts of God as Creator and His gifts as Father, or between His creation gifts and His redemption gifts. God indeed gives certain gifts (harvest, babies, food, life, breath, rain, He makes His sun rise on the just and the unjust alike, Matthew 5:45) whether people pray or not, whether they believe or not.

However, God's redemption gifts are different. God does not bestow salvation on all alike, but He bestows his riches upon all who call on Him (Romans 10:12-13). The same applies to post-salvation blessings. When Jesus refers to *good things or what is good* in verse 11, He is referring to spiritual gifts (daily forgiveness, deliverance from evil, peace, the increase of faith, hope, and love, in fact, the indwelling work of the Holy Spirit) and not material blessings. The Lord's prayer brings together both kinds of gifts.

Why do we pray for daily bread, and how can both the material and spiritual blessings be prayed for in the same prayer? The answer may be this. We pray for daily bread not because we fear we will starve otherwise (since millions get their bread without even praying for it or saying grace before meals) but because we know that ultimately it comes from God and because, as his children, it is appropriate to acknowledge our physical dependence on Him regularly. However, we pray for forgiveness and deliverance because these gifts are given only in answer to prayer and because we would be lost without them. So, prayer is not unnecessary.

Prayer is Unproductive:

This problem is closely related to the second problem. Some agree prayer is unnecessary because God gives to many who do not ask. It is unproductive because He fails to provide for many who do. "I prayed to pass an exam but failed it. I asked God to heal a friend or family member, but He did not heal them. I prayed for peace, but the world fills with the noise of war. Prayer doesn't work!"

The best way to answer this problem is to remember the promises of Jesus concerning prayer are not unconditional. With every promise, there is a premise! In other words, you cannot ask God to help you pass a test if you have not first studied for the test. We are notorious for asking God to do things for us, which first requires some responsibility for us.

If we think about this for one minute, we will realize its truth. It is absurd to suppose the promise *Ask and it will be given to you* is an absolute pledge with no strings attached; that *Knock, and it will be opened to you* is an "Open, Sesame" to every closed door without exception; and that by the waving of a prayer wand, God will grant any wish, and every dream will come true. The idea is ridiculous. It would turn prayer into magic and God into our servant who appears instantly to do our bidding like Aladdin's genie whenever we rub our little prayer lamp. In addition, it would place significant stress on every Christian. One author said if this were the case, he would never pray again because he would not have sufficient confidence in his own wisdom to ask God for anything. It would impose an intolerable burden on frail human understanding if, by His promises, God pledged to give him anything he asked for. How could we bear such a burden?

Remember, with every promise, there is a premise. In other words, certain conditions must be met before God will answer our prayers.

Here are some of those conditions from a Biblical point of view:

BIBLE TEXT	CONDITION for EFFECTIVE PRAYER
Matthew 21:22; 11:24	You must believe.
John 14:13-14; 15:16; 16:33	You must pray "in Jesus Name."
I Peter 3:7	You must treat your wife properly.
Ephesians 5:17	You must understand God's Will.
Romans 1:10	You must depend on God's Will.
John 15:7; 15:10	You must abide in Christ.
Psalm 66:18	You must have no unconfessed sin.
Psalm 37:4	You must love (delight in) the Lord.
I John 5:14-15	You must pray in the Lord's will.

Being good, our Father gives only good gifts to His children; being wise also, He knows which gifts are good and which are not. We have already heard Jesus say that human parents would never give a stone or snake to their children who ask for bread or fish. But what if the children (through ignorance or folly), were to ask for a stone to eat or a snake to eat? What then? Some irresponsible parents might grant the request, but most parents would be too wise and loving to do so. Our heavenly Father would never give us anything harmful, even if we ask for it urgently and repeatedly.

We can be thankful that the granting of our needs is conditional, not only on our asking, seeking, and knocking but also on whether what we desire is good and in the will of God for us. Thank God he answers prayer. Thank God He sometimes denies our requests.

The Product of Prayer:

The *Therefore* of verse 12 is very important. It may look back to the previous verse and imply that since God is good to all who seek Him in prayer, his children must therefore seek Him in prayer. It may also refer back to the *Judge not* command and take up the underlying argument against hypocrisy (Not judging the splinter in another's eye without removing the beam from my eye). Jesus uttered this principle at different times in different contexts. For example, Luke's version of the Sermon on the Mount, it comes after the three little cameos, which illustrate the command to love our enemies (Luke 6:31). Certainly, such love is beyond us, apart from the grace of God. It is, in fact, His love and is one of the *good things* He gives us through His Holy Spirit in answer to our prayers.

In this context, God takes care of the needs of His people and withholds the things that are not good for them or those who do not meet the requirements of His will in their lives. That is how we want God to treat us and how we should treat others around us. This kind of care is part of the character

234

of God, which He tells us to copy, indeed, become the character of God here on earth.

Conclusion:

What are the lessons we learn? First, we discovered that prayer presupposes some things. It presupposes knowledge of God's will for us. We must take pains to find it through Scripture, meditation, and the exercise of the Christian mind schooled in such reflection. It also presupposes faith. It is one thing to know God's will, but another to humble ourselves before Him and express our confidence that He can bring His will to fulfillment.

Prayer also presupposes desire. We may know God's will, believe He can perform it, and still not desire it. Therefore, prayer is the chief means God ordained to express our deepest desires. For this reason, we ask, seek, and knock. Thus, before we ask, we must know what to ask for and whether it accords with God's will; we must believe God can grant it, and genuinely want to receive it. Then the gracious promises of Jesus will come true.

The second lesson is that if we do not receive answers to prayer immediately, we should persevere in prayer until we do or until God shows us that the petition is not according to His will. That is the purpose of these present imperatives (commands).

Third, we learn as we keep praying, God keeps working on our behalf. Many a meager Christian experience is due to a meager prayer life.

Finally, we learn we have no right to demand of God that He answers our prayer, but we may keep on reverently knocking with the hand of faith.

Review and Resolve:

1. What is the significance of the repetition of asking, seeking, and knocking?
2. What is the principle Jesus teaches with the "stone" and "snake" illustrations?
3. Why do people raise problems or objections to the promises of Jesus?
4. What is the best answer to the objection that prayer is unproductive?
5. Explain the principle "With every Promise, there is a Premise."
6. What part of this lesson did you appreciate the most?
7. Name a few things that you learn from this discussion.

Chapter 28

The Narrow Gate

Enter by the narrow gate; for the gate is wide, and the way is broad that leads to destruction, and many are those who enter by it. For the gate is small, and the way is narrow that leads to life, and few are those who find it. Beware of the false prophets, who come to you in sheep's clothing, but inwardly are ravenous wolves. You will know them by their fruits. Grapes are not gathered from thorn bushes, nor figs from thistles, are they? Even so, every good tree bears good fruit; but the bad tree bears bad fruit. A good tree cannot produce bad fruit, nor can a bad tree produce good fruit. Every tree that does not bear good fruit is cut down and thrown into the fire. So then, you will know them by their fruits. Not everyone who says to Me, 'Lord, Lord,' will enter the kingdom of heaven; but he who does the will of My Father who is in heaven. Many will say to Me on that day, 'Lord, Lord, did we not prophesy in Your name, and in Your name cast out demons, and in Your name perform many miracles?' And then I will declare to them, I never knew you; 'DEPART FROM ME, YOU WHO PRACTICE LAWLESSNESS.' (Matthew 7:13-23)

Life always carries a dramatic quality, as it has been said, "... all life concentrates on man at the crossroads." Every action of life confronts man with a choice; and he can never evade the choice, because he can never stand still. He must always take one way or the other. Because of that, it has always been one of the supreme functions of the great men of history that they should confront men with that inevitable choice.

As the end drew near, Moses spoke to the people: *See, I have set before you this day life and good, and death and evil... Therefore, choose life, that you and your seed may live* (Deuteronomy 30:15-20).

When Joshua laid down the nation's leadership at the end of his life, he gave them the same choice: *"Choose you this day whom you will serve"* (Joshua 24:15).

Jeremiah heard the voice of God saying to him, *unto this people shall you say, thus says the Lord: 'Behold I have set before you the way of life and the way of death'* (Jeremiah 21:8).

In this passage, we have come to the end of the main body of Jesus' sermon (or His teaching) and now the application or conclusion begins. In this application, Jesus places the same kind of choice before all who would read these words. He emphasizes the necessity for choice in the lives of people. When he talks about the narrow gate and the broad way, He contrasts the two kinds of righteousness, the two treasures, the two masters, and the two ambitions. Now the time for a decision has come. Is it to be the kingdom of Satan or the kingdom of God, the prevailing culture or the Christian counterculture? Jesus continues with His presentation of the alternative as He describes the two ways (broad and narrow), the two teachers (false and true), the two pleas (words and deeds), and finally, the two foundations (sand and rock).

As we observe Christ's teaching to those entering the kingdom, we will see what He warns them to beware of. You and I face certain issues every day of our Christian life and He speaks to some of them here.

Beware of Broad Crowded Ways (Matthew 7:13-14).

What is immediately striking about these verses is the absolute nature of choice. All of us would rather have more options than only one. Some turned down all choices and created a conglomerate religion that eliminated the need for choice. But Jesus cuts across our easy-going syncretism. He will not allow us the comfortable solutions we propose. Instead, He insists there is only one choice because there are only two possibilities. It will help us to observe from these two verses just what Jesus says we should choose from.

There are Two Ways:

This concept is found already in the Old Testament in Psalm 1, which contrasts the way of the righteous and the way of the ungodly. In this passage, Jesus elaborates on the picture in the first Psalm.

Jesus says the way is broad and this word means *broad, spacious, roomy.* Some manuscripts combine these images and call this way *wide and easy.* There is plenty of room for diversity of opinions and laxity of morals. It is the road of tolerance and permissiveness, and it has no curbstones, no boundaries of either thought or conduct. Travelers on this road follow their inclinations, that of the desires of their hearts, even though those hearts are in a fallen condition. Superficiality, self-love, hypocrisy, mechanical religion, false ambition, and censoriousness do not have to be learned or cultivated. An effort is needed to resist them. No effect is required to practice them, and that is why this road is broad.

However, there is a narrow and hard way. Its boundaries are marked, and its narrowness is due to "Divine Revelation," which restricts pilgrims to the confines of what God has revealed in Scripture to be accurate and sound. It is a fact that revealed truth imposes a limitation on what Christians may believe and revealed goodness on how we may behave. In one sense, it is hard, but in another sense, we are to regard it as Christ's *easy yoke* and *a light burden* (Matthew 11:30).

There are Two Gates:

The gate leading to the broad way is "wide," which makes it a simple matter to get on the broad road, and evidently, there is no limit to the luggage a person may take with him. Therefore, we need not leave anything behind, not even our sins, self-righteousness, or pride.

The gate leading to the narrow road is also narrow. One has to look for it to find it. We can miss it. Jesus suggested in another place that it was as small as a needle's eye. Further, to enter it, we must leave everything behind: sin, selfish ambition, covetousness, even if necessary, family and friends. For none can follow Christ who has not first denied himself. This gate is like a turnpike gate––we must enter individually. How can we find it? It is Jesus Christ Himself! *I am the door, if anyone enters by Me, he will be saved* (John 10:9).

There are Two Destinations:

Psalm 1 foreshadows two destinations in the *Prospering* and the *Perishing*." These are the two alternatives. Moses made it more explicit in Deuteronomy when he said, *See, I have set before you this day life and good, death and evil... blessing and curse; therefore, choose life"* (Deuteronomy 30:15, 19). Similarly, Jesus taught that the broad way and wide gate lead to *destruction*. This word means *destruction, waste, loss, perishing*. This verse makes the unique sense of the loss of eternal life.

By contrast, the hard way, entered by the narrow gate, leads to life, precisely that of eternal life. Jesus explains this in terms of fellowship with God, beginning here, but perfected hereafter, in which we see and share His glory and find perfect fulfillment as human beings in Him and selflessly serving our fellows.

There are Two Crowds:

The broad and easy road is a busy thoroughfare, thronged by pedestrians of every kind. However, the narrow and hard way leading to life seems to be comparatively deserted. *Those who find it are few.* Jesus seems to have anticipated that His followers might feel themselves to be a despised minority movement. He saw multitudes on the broad road, laughing and carefree with apparently no thought for the dreadful end to which they were heading. In contrast, while on the narrow road He saw only a few pilgrims with backs turned on sin and faces set toward the Celestial City.

In these verses, Jesus draws these contrasts in two ways, two gates, two crowds, and two destinations. It is hardly necessary to comment that such talk is extremely unfashionable today. People like to be uncommitted. Every opinion poll allows not only for a "yes" or "no" answer but for convenience "undecided." To deviate from the middle way is to risk being dubbed an "extremist" or a "fanatic." Everybody resists facing the necessity of choice. But Jesus will not allow us to escape it.

Beware of False Teachers (Matthew 7:15-20).

The Assumption:

Jesus assumed there would be such people in His kingdom. There is no sense in putting up the "Beware of Dog" sign on your fence if all you have is a sleepy pussy cat. Jesus warned His followers of false prophets because they already existed. We see it on numerous occasions in the Old Testament, and Jesus seems to have regarded the Pharisees and the Sadducees in the same light. *Blind leaders leading the blind,* He called them. He also implied they would increase, and the rise of false teachers leading many astray would characterize the period preceding the end. Matthew 24:11-14 also predicts the worldwide spread of the gospel.

We hear of them in nearly every New Testament letter. They are called either "pseudo-prophets" as here (prophets presumably because they claim divine inspiration), "pseudo-apostles" (because they claimed apostolic authority, II Corinthians 11:13), or "pseudo-teachers" (II Peter 2:1) or even "pseudo-Christs" (because they made messianic pretensions or denied that Jesus was the Christ come in the flesh, Matthew 24:24; Mark 13:22; I John 2:18, 22). But each was "pseudo," and this word is the Greek word for a lie. The history of the Christian church has been a long and dreary story of controversy with false teachers. Their value in the overruling providence of God is that they have presented the church with a challenge to think out and define the truth, but they have caused much damage. Unfortunately, I fear there are still many in today's church.

There is another assumption, namely that there is such a thing as an objective standard of truth from which the falsehood of the false prophet is to be distinguished. The very notion of false prophets is meaningless otherwise.

The Warnings:

Jesus says, *Beware of the false prophets, who come to you in sheep's clothing, but inwardly are ravenous wolves.* We learn from this metaphorical description that pseudo-prophets are dangerous and deceptive.

Their danger is that, in reality, they are "wolves." In first-century Palestine, the wolf was the natural enemy of sheep, entirely defenseless against it. Hence a good shepherd, as Jesus was to teach later (John 10:11-13), was always on the lookout for wolves to protect his sheep. Just like sheep, Christ's flock is at the mercy of good shepherds, paid laborers, or wolves. The good pastor feeds the community with the truth. The false teacher, like a wolf, divides it by error. At the same time, the timeserving professional does nothing to protect it but abandons it to false teachers. So, Paul said in Acts 20:29-30 to the Ephesian elders, *I know that after my departure fierce wolves will come in among you, not sparing the flock; and from among your own selves will arise men speaking perverse things to draw away the disciples after them. Therefore, be on the alert ....*

It is no accident Jesus' warns about false prophets in the Sermon on the Mount immediately following His teaching about the two gates, ways, crowds, and destinations. False prophets are adept at blurring the issue of salvation. Some so muddle or distort the gospel that they make it hard for seekers to find the narrow gate. Others teach that the narrow way is, in reality, much broader than Jesus implied and that to walk on it requires little, if any, restriction on one's belief or behavior. Perhaps the most pernicious dare to contradict Jesus and assert the broad road does not lead to destruction, but still, all roads lead to God, and even the broad and narrow roads, although they lead off in opposite directions, ultimately both end in life. We must remember the words of Jesus in John 14:6, *I am the way, the truth, and the life. No one comes to the Father but through Me.*

No wonder Jesus likened such false teachers to *ravenous wolves,* not so much because they are greedy for gain, prestige, and power (though they often are), but because they are "ferocious" (NIV), that is, extremely dangerous. They are responsible for leading some people to the destruction they say does not exist.

But they are more than dangerous; they are deceptive. Because of their dirty habits, the "dogs" and "pigs" of verse 6 are easy to recognize. Because they look like sheep, the flock welcomes them. But, often it is discovered too late, and they already did their damage.

These false teachers do not announce and advertise themselves as a purveyor of lies. On the contrary, they claim to be teachers of the truth. Not only do they pretend piety, but they often use the language of historic orthodoxy to gain acceptance from the gullible while meaning by it something entirely different, something destructive of the truth they pretend to hold. Also, often they hide behind the cover of high-sounding titles and impressive academic degrees.

So, Jesus warns, "Beware!" We must be on our guard, pray for discernment, use our critical faculties, and never relax our vigilance. We must not be dazzled by a person's outer clothing, charm, learning, doctorates, or ecclesiastical honors. Instead, we must look under the outward appearance to reality. What lives under the fleece: a sheep or a wolf?

The Tests:

Now Jesus changes His metaphor from sheep and wolves to trees and their fruit. In so doing, He moved from the risk of non-recognition to the means of recognition. It may be possible to mistake a wolf for a sheep, but you cannot make the same mistake with a tree. No tree can hide its identity for long. Sooner or later, it betrays itself by its fruit. A wolf may disguise itself, but a tree cannot. Noxious weeds like thorns and thistles cannot produce edible fruit like grapes and figs. Not only is the character of the fruit determined by the tree (a fig tree bearing figs and vine grapes), but its condition too (every sound tree bears good fruit, but a bad tree bears evil fruit, (v. 17). Indeed, a good tree cannot bear evil fruit, nor can a bad tree bear good fruit (v. 18). And the day of judgment will finalize the difference, as when non-fruit-bearing trees are cut down and burned (v. 19). Therefore (for this is the conclusion which Jesus emphasizes twice) "you will know them by their fruits (v. 16, 20). Therefore, the first and primary test is the fruit that a person bears.

First, it is the character and manner of life of the prophet. It is character and conduct. It is the "fruit of the Spirit." When we see the meekness and gentleness of Christ, His love, patience, kindness, goodness, and self-control, we have reason to believe Him to be true, not false. On the other hand, when we see enmity, impurity, jealousy, and self-indulgence, we are justified in suspecting that the prophet is an impostor, however pretentious his claims and specious his teaching.

Second, it is the man's actual teaching. In the same fruit-tree metaphor, Jesus strongly suggests the other use: *The tree is known by its fruit. You brood of vipers! How can you speak good, when you are evil? For out of the abundance of the heart the mouth speaks. The good man out of his good treasure brings forth good, and the evil man out of his evil treasure brings forth evil. I tell you, on the day of judgment men will render account for every careless word they utter; for by your words you will be justified, and by your words you will be condemned"* (Matthew 12:33-37; Luke 6:45). So then, if a person's heart is revealed by his words, as a tree is known by its fruit, we have a responsibility to test a teacher by his teaching.

Therefore, Jesus warns us to examine a teacher's credentials, character, conduct, and message.

Review and Resolve:

1. What contrast is Jesus making when He uses the concept of the narrow gate and the broad way?
2. What are some implications of the "broad road?"
3. What do you think and feel about the choices Jesus offers in this passage?
4. What two assumptions does Jesus make regarding false prophets?
5. What is the implication of *ravenous wolves?*
6. What is the first test of a false or true prophet?
7. By what standard do we check a man's teaching?
8. Can you give an account of an encounter with a false teacher?

Chapter 29

Beware of Superficial Religion

Not everyone who says to Me, 'Lord, Lord,' will enter the kingdom of heaven; but he who does the will of My Father who is in heaven. Many will say to Me on that day, 'Lord, Lord, did we not prophesy in Your name, and in Your name cast out demons, and in Your name perform many miracles?' And then I will declare to them, 'I never knew you; DEPART FROM ME, YOU WHO PRACTICE LAWLESSNESS.' Therefore everyone who hears these words of Mine, and acts upon them, may be compared to a wise man, who built his house upon the rock. And the rain descended, and the floods came, and the winds blew, and burst against that house; and yet it did not fall, for it had been founded upon the rock. And everyone who hears these words of Mine, and does not act upon them, will be like a foolish man, who built his house upon the sand. 'And the rain descended, and the floods came, and the winds blew, and burst against that house; and it fell, and great was its fall' (Matthew 7:21-27).

A Short Review:

When we began this passage, we said it is the conclusion of the Lord Jesus to His Sermon on the Mount. He warns the people who will live in His kingdom against some of the issues which could lead them astray.

First, He points out that the only way to enter the kingdom is through a narrow, small gate onto a narrow road. Then we saw Jesus Himself as the gate (John 10:9). That is the choice we must make at sometime or other in our lives.

Jesus then proceeded to tell us to beware of false teachers. He places this warning in proper sequence because He knew there would be those teachers who would teach the broad road was the one that leads to salvation. He knew these false teachers would be responsible for leading some people to the very destruction which they would say did not exist. When Jesus changed His metaphor from sheep and wolves to trees and their fruit, He moved from the risk of non-recognition to the means of recognition. Therefore, He gave us tests by which we can recognize false teachers.

A Last Warning:

Now He continues to warn us against deceptions available to us in the kingdom. One is superficial religion, and the last is the risk of building a foundation that will not hold up in the storm.

Without question, Jesus begins His conclusion and application in verse 13. J. C. Ryle said about these passages: "The Lord Jesus winds up the Sermon on the Mount by a passage of heart-piercing application. He turns from false prophets to false professors, from unsound teachers to unsound hearers." In other words, it is not only false teachers who make the narrow way hard to find and difficult to tread. A man may also be grievously self-deceived. Some people think they are in the kingdom, while all the time, they are not. Let's look at the passage:

Beware of Superficial Religion (Matthew 7:21-23).

The people Jesus describes here rely for salvation on a creedal affirmation of what they say to or about Christ. Jesus insists that our final destiny will be settled, neither by what we say to Him today nor by what we shall say to Him on the last day, but by whether we *do* what we say. Considering this concept becomes terrifying for every person, especially professing Christians. The destiny of every person will be determined on the basis of whether the verbal profession is accompanied by moral obedience.

A verbal profession is necessary. Paul stated that clearly in Romans 10:9-10. Furthermore, we learn from I Corinthians 12:3 that the true profession of Jesus as Lord is impossible without the Holy Spirit. At least on the surface, the Christian confession Jesus describes is wholly admirable. Notice that these people call Jesus "Lord" four times. Also notice that they prophesy, cast out demons, and perform many miracles in His name. This profession is polite, it is orthodox, it is fervent and it is public. It is even spectacular at times. To make His point, Jesus cites the most extreme examples of the verbal profession, namely the exercise of supernatural ministry involving prophecy, exorcism, and miracles. These people stress the name in which they ministered. They use it thrice, and each time they put it first for emphasis.

There are some tremendous permanent truths and principles in this passage. Looking at them carefully and understanding them could change the way some of us live and put us into lockstep with the will of Christ for our lives. But first, it will help us to look at these truths:

There is only one way a man's sincerity can be proved: by his practice-- the way he lives his life.

Fine words can never be a substitute for fine deeds. There is only one proof, and that is obedience. There is no point in saying we love a person, and then doing things that break that person's heart. We might hear a child say to his mother, "Mother, I love you." But we might sometimes hear the mother say, "I wish you would show it a little more in how you behave." So often, we confess God with our lips and deny Him with our lives. It is not difficult to recite a creed, but it is challenging to live the Christian life. Faith without practice is a contradiction of terms, and love without obedience is an impossibility.

Success, as the world counts it, is not a criterion of one's knowledge of Christ and a relationship with Him.

The people about whom Jesus speaks cite their successes, and it appears these were accepted by the world around them. There were many who believed in them and thought they were the most wonderful ministers who ever lived. That was because they heard them prophesy in Jesus' name, and they saw them cast out demons and perform miracles in Jesus' name. However, success is not the criterion for attempting to determine if a person is moral or even saved for that matter. We must remember the words of Isaiah 55:1: *So shall My word be which goes forth from My mouth; it shall not return to Me empty (void).* Also, in Matthew 24:35, Jesus said, *Heaven and earth shall pass away, but My word shall not pass away.* The Word of God will always do its work, which cannot be stopped even by the devil himself.

It is easy to look at the great buildings which some preachers have built. It is easy to fall under the teaching of men who seem to have the truth. It is a simple matter of getting caught up in the principles which some preachers teach, and it is not uncommon to have our lives changed because of their teaching. However, that is not the basis for determining whether they are moral or Godly. We must closely observe their character and their lives. What do we know about them? Once we do our homework, often we find that they are not worth our audience, let alone our allegiance.

The idea of judgement is at the back of this passage.

All through it, there runs the certainty that the day of reckoning is coming. A man may succeed for a long time in maintaining the pretenses and the disguises. Still, there comes a day when the pretenses are shown for what they are, and the disguises strip away. We may deceive men with our words, but we cannot fool God. Psalm 139:2 says of God, *You know when I sit down and when I rise up; you understand my thought from afar.* No man can ultimately deceive God, who sees everything, especially man's heart.

In verse 23, Jesus says that in the time of judgment, *I will declare.* The word for *declare* or *confess* is the very word that is used in Matthew 10:32, which says, *Everyone therefore who shall <u>confess</u> Me before men, I will also <u>confess</u> him before My Father who is in heaven.* Christ's confession to them will be like theirs in being public, but unlike theirs, it will be true. This public and open announcement spells their doom.

Their rejection by Him is because their profession was verbal, not moral. It concerned their lips only and not their lives. It was talk without truth, profession without reality. They called Him *Lord, Lord,* but never submitted to His Lordship or obeyed the will of His Heavenly Father. The vital difference is between "saying" and "doing." Christ the Judge will banish them from His presence because they are *evildoers.* They may claim to do "mighty works" in their ministry, but in their everyday behavior, their works are not good but evil. The result? They must hear those awesome and awful words, *I never knew you; depart from Me, you who practice lawlessness.* Beware of a Fair-Weather Foundation (Matthew 7:24-27).

In these final words of Jesus, He is making a different contrast. In the previous verses, the difference was between "saying" and "doing." In this passage, the distinction is between "hearing" and "doing." On the one hand, Jesus says, there is the person who *Hears these words of mine and does them* (v. 24), and on the other hand, the person who *hears these words of mine and does not do them* (v. 26). He then illustrates the contrast between His obedient and disobedient hearers by His well-known parable of the two builders. He may have Proverbs 10:25 in mind as the basis of His illustration: *When the whirlwind passes, the wicked is no more, But the righteous has an everlasting foundation.*

251

As these two builders proceeded with their buildings, a casual observer would not have noticed any difference. The difference was in the foundations, and foundations are generally not seen. The foundation and fatal difference revealed themselves only when a storm broke and battered both houses. The house on the rock withstood the gale, while the house on the sand collapsed in irreparable ruin.

Jesus demanded that men should LISTEN. One of the great difficulties facing us today is a simple fact that men often do not know what Jesus said or what the church teaches. The matter is worse. They usually have a mistaken notion of what Jesus said. It is not honest to condemn a person (Jesus Christ) until he understands what that person stands for, came from, or what He has said. Therefore, the first step in the Christian life is to give Jesus Christ a chance to speak. Once we know what He says, we build a foundation in our Christian lives. And without that foundation, we will never be able to conduct our lives as God desires. Every time a storm comes into our lives, we will crumble. What Jesus says is in His Word, the Bible.

Jesus also demanded that men should DO. Knowledge only becomes relevant when it translates into action. It would be possible for a person to pass an examination in Christian Ethics with the highest grade, and yet not be a Christian. Knowledge must become action; theory must become practice; theology must become life lived daily. There is little point in going to the doctor unless we are prepared to do the things we hear him say to us. Yet, thousands of people listen to the teaching of Jesus every Sunday, have excellent knowledge of what He taught, and yet make little or no deliberate attempt to put it into practice.

Conclusion:

The truth Jesus is insisting in these final two paragraphs of the Sermon on the Mount is that neither an intellectual knowledge of Him nor a verbal profession, though both are essential in themselves, can be a substitute for obedience. The question is not whether we say nice, polite, orthodox, enthusiastic things to or about Jesus; nor whether we hear His words, listening, studying, pondering, and memorizing until we stuff our minds with His teaching; but whether we do what we say and do what we know. In other words, whether the Lordship of Jesus, which we profess, is one of our life's significant realities.

Thomas a' Kempis said centuries ago, "Instant obedience is the only kind of obedience there is; delayed obedience is disobedience. Whoever strives to withdraw from obedience, withdraws from Grace."

The entire issue of the Sermon on the Mount is to do precisely and only what it says to do. It is all about doing. It is much easier to do what God gives us to do, no matter how hard it is, than to face the responsibilities of not doing it.

Review and Resolve:

1. How would you define "superficial religion?"
2. What is the relationship between the verbal profession of Christ and moral obedience to Christ?
3. Can you give an example of someone who had success, as the world counts it, but did not have a relationship with Christ?
4. How should those terrifying words of Jesus, *"I never knew you; depart from Me, you who practice lawlessness,"* affect how we live our lives?
5. Describe the importance of our foundation in the Christian faith.
6. How can we get a proper foundation for our Christian lives?
7. What do you think of the statement in our lesson, "Knowledge must become action; theory must become practice; theology must become life?"

Author Biography

Richard Hagenbaugh was born into a small coal mining community in Northeastern Pennsylvania, where life was hard. His mother died when he was two, and his father became a severe alcoholic. Richard struggled in school and quit at one point. When he was nineteen, he turned his life over to Christ, giving him the urgency to be God's man.

After high school, he joined the Air Force. Following training and Top-Secret security clearance, the military sent him to Anchorage, Alaska, where he met and married Carolyn. They landed on their feet doing ministry, their continuing life's focus.

Richard's next military assignment was on the island of Taiwan, where he was privileged to preach in a working leprosarium. That ministry gave him a love for people, especially those in the most desperate circumstances. He led an evangelistic ministry among Chinese university students and helped to start a church. God used the Taiwan experience to convince him of His call into ministry.

He received a BA in Bible, an MDiv, then a DMin in 1987. He pastored Aims Community Church for five years and Gateway Baptist for the next thirty years. During that time, he experienced every form of difficulty a church could encounter: murders, suicides, child abuse, and domestic disturbance. In addition to church and staff issues, his family was threatened once with a gun. After Rich was in ministry for about eight years, one seasoned pastor said, *I have been in ministry for forty years and have never encountered the things you have.* Nevertheless, Rich always believed he was right where God wanted him and would equip him for whatever He chose to bring.

After illness and forced retirement, he and Carolyn went to North Idaho to recoup. Eventually, his health improved, and he was interim in three churches over eight years and significantly impacted all three. After some fifty years in Pastoral Ministry, he serves his local church as an elder, is part of the preaching team, leads a small group, and shepherds several dozen people. His driving force in ministry is that only two things on the planet last for eternity, **God's Word** and **People.** Therefore, he has dedicated his life to the exposition of the Bible and loving and ministering to people.

Bibliography

Allen, Charles L., *The Sermon on the Mount,* Fleming H. Revell Company, Westwood, New Jersey, 1966.

Barclay, William, *The Gospel of Matthew, Volume 1,* The Westminster Press, Philadelphia, Pennsylvania, 1958.

Boice, James Montgomery, *The Sermon on the Mount,* Zondervan Publishing House, Grand Rapids, Michigan, 1972.

Broadus, John A. D.D. L.L.D., *Commentary on the Gospel of Matthew,* The Judson Press, Valley Forge, Pennsylvania, 1886.

Edersheim, Alfred, *The Life and Times of Jesus the Messiah,* William B. Eerdmans, Publishing Company, Grand Rapids, Michigan, 1969.

Fruchtenbaum, Arnold G., *Yeshua, The Life of Messiah, From a Messianic Jewish Perspective,* Published by Ariel Ministries, San Antonio, Texas, 2019.

Guelich, Robert A., *The Sermon on the Mount, A Foundation for Understanding,* World Books Publishers, Waco, Texas, 1982.

Hendriksen, William, *New Testament Commentary, Exposition of the Gospel According to Matthew,* Baker Book House, Grand Rapids, Michigan, 1973.

Lloyd-Jones, D. Martyn, *Studies in The Sermon on the Mount,* Wm. B. Eerdmans Publishing Company, Grand Rapids, Michigan, 1960.

Pink, Arthur W., *An Exposition on the Sermon on the Mount,* Baker Book House, Grand Rapids, Michigan, 1962.

Thompson, Ernest Trice, *The Sermon on the Mount, and its meaning for Today,* John Knox Press, Richmond, Virginia, 1953.

Walvoord, John F., *Matthew, Thy Kingdom Come,* Moody Press, Chicago, Illinois, 1974.

Printed in the USA
CPSIA information can be obtained
at www.ICGtesting.com
JSHW010240311023
51155JS00004B/7